Praise for Jacquie Jordan

"Jacquie Jordan was the first television producer to put me and my first book on the air. The episode Jacquie produced opened the door to many more TV interviews and now that my second book, Traveling Hopefully, has become a bestseller, I use the principles she taught me every time I go on TV."

—Libby Gill, personal coach and author of *Traveling Hopefully: How to Lose Your Family Baggage and Jumpstart Your Life*

"*Get on TV* is a must-read for anybody who has even the faintest desire to appear on a television show. Jacquie's experience, combined with her down-to-earth approach, makes the information real and applicable in a format that is easy to digest, and can get you booked on TV."

—Colleen Wyse, Associate Publisher, *Jane Magazine*

"Now that I've read Jacquie's book, I've got a gazillion and one ideas on marketing the 'Cody Product' and a gazillion and fourteen ideas about the wacky travel show. I started a new radio weather gig today and I think it's going to be *huge*.... They want me to be more of a co-host than just a weather guy, and it's a blast."

—Cody Stark, Weather Anchor/TV Host, KOVR 13, Sacramento, CA

"Everything Jacquie writes about talking to TV producers and talk show hosts is right on target and was extremely helpful in helping me promote my book *Maneater* on TV (CNN, Portland, Seattle, San Francisco). The paperback version to be published in the fall by St. Martin's Press will be called *The Woman with the Worm in Her Head.*"

—Pam Nagami, MD

"Jacquie Jordan writes with humor and humility about the often chaotic and hectic pace of television producing and lets the reader in on knowing how important they are to the show and the process."

—Marla Maples

Get on TV!

The Insider's Guide to Pitching the Producers and Promoting Yourself

Jacquie Jordan
Foreword by Donny Osmond

SOURCEBOOKS, INC.®
NAPERVILLE, ILLINOIS

Published by Sourcebooks, Inc.
P.O. Box 4410, Naperville, Illinois   60567-4410
(630) 961-3900
fax: (630) 961-2168
www.sourcebooks.com

Library of Congress Cataloging-in-Publication Data

Jordan, Jacquie.
  Get on TV! : the insider's guide to pitching the producers and promoting yourself /
Jacquie Jordan.
     p. cm.
  ISBN-13: 978-1-4022-0591-0
  ISBN-10: 1-4022-0591-0
  1. Talk shows. 2. Reality television programs. 3. Television in publicity. I. Title.

PN1992.8.T3J67 2006
791.45'6--dc22

                                                    2005025007

Printed and bound in the United States of America.
          VP   10 9 8 7 6 5 4 3 2

Contents

Acknowledgments

I had no idea it would have taken so many people's support during the process of writing a book on a subject that is second nature to me. I am truly humbled. I thought writing a book was a one-man job, how wrong was I!

To Patrick Smith, for the year that changed my life personally and professionally—every day I am grateful. To my parents, Jackie and Dennis Petruzzelli, and my siblings, Stephanie and Justin. The four little ones—Morgan, Abbie, Olivia, and Collin. My grandma, Maria Lindblom, and Howard Skinner, cousin Jordan Mallari, Aunt Sue (my other mother), and significantly Brett Shapoff.

Susan Gold for making the introductions to Monique Raphel High, my book proposal muse, and Mark Parsons, my secret weapon. To Greg Lyons and Jeff Brenner for moving the caboose.

My literary agent, Kirsten Manges at Curtis Brown Ltd.; my editor Peter Lynch and the supportive folks at Sourcebooks; and for the photo—Starla Fortunato.

Thank you to Randi Paige, Sharon Lindsey, Jackie Hakim, Kay Ostberg, Giuditta Tornetta, Linda Avarites, and Diana Jahre—sisters of choice. And to Loretta Sparks, the Wise-Witch, everyone should have one of you in their lives.

The folks along the way: Dick Sutphen, Tara Sutphen, Bart Smith, Kathy Giaconia, Charlie Cook, Maureen Fitzpatrick, Marty Casas, Marcia Wilke, Angelica Holiday, Dawn Holman, Joe Scott, Robert Kosberg, Stan Corwin, Libby Gill, Heather and Susie DeWeese, Michaela Starr, Brian Lowry, and Debbie Luican.

Especially: Scott Sternberg and the great staff and experience at *Sunday Morning Shootout*, again Susan Gold, and Jackie Hakim, Stacey Davis Jackson, AJ Lewis, Kevin Scarboro, Melissa Chase, Martineque McClain, Johnny Casas, Robin Felson Von Halle, Bill Whittle, and of course Peter Guber and Peter Bart.

The talent, guests, clients, and colleagues I've had the privilege to work with who have a proven vision invaluable to the work: Jonathon Fong, Sonya Nimri, Cheryl Sindell, Anthony V. Salerno, Eddie Conner, Pete Siegel, Dyanna St. James, Tara Aranson, Susie Mains, Mary Spio, Scott Lewis, Letha Hadady, Michelle Lee Flores, Don Herron, Anat Baron, Jill Sanborne, and the rest...may your TV dreams come true! I hope this book will prove to be an invaluable stepping-stone on your path.

Foreword

It is three minutes before the start of the *Donny & Marie* show. The audience is in place, the crew is on standby, and the lights have been brought up. As usual, I am pacing backstage going over the material in my head for today's taping. The band starts to play the theme song. Jacquie Jordan is standing by the stage entrance wearing her headset and holding a clipboard full of scripts, notes, and guest information. It represents the hours of preparation that have gone into this upcoming moment. As the stage manager cues me, Jacquie reminds me to get the guest's plug into the segment before throwing to the tape package that plays before the commercial break. And you thought a talk show was just the hosts and guests chatting, right?

I've been performing since the age of five, when I learned to sing and dance along with my brothers for *The Andy Williams Show.* When I became a talk show host in 1998 for *Donny & Marie,* I entered a whole new world, not one of memorizing dance steps and lyrics, but one that requires knowing names and remembering facts and backgrounds (while remaining present to the ins and outs from commercial breaks, time cues, conversation flow, and, oh yes, paying attention to what the guest is actually saying). I never had homework like this when I was a kid! And after the first taping of each day, there will be another round of information to absorb for another show taping that same day.

A good talk show has to have a good producer who brings together the content, guests, and material for the show. Speaking as one of the hosts, as prepared as I would be for a taping, there is a lot less pressure on me if the guests know how to be great guests—interesting, talkative, enthusiastic, and knowledgeable. A huge burden rests on the shoulders of the producer: to supply great guests. So it's essential to have one who is both creative and organized—as is Jacquie Jordan.

In *Get on TV!*, Jacquie illustrates the need for new ideas, stories, and personalities and where the producer's search for quality guests begins and ends. Her down-to-earth candor is as real and refreshing in its approach as I've found Jacquie to be. With her "I'm-one-of-you" style of writing, she conveys the fundamental how-to-do-it-yourself message and makes it clear that the *show is only as good as the guests.*

Donny Osmond

Introduction ⋁

We, the television producers, want you! We're looking for you. We're looking for new ideas, new faces, all the time. Ultimately, that is what we make a living doing. We package and sell ideas, people, and concepts to a mass viewer.

It's about connection. This book is going to tell you how to connect with us, and how to get into our Rolodex, so ultimately, you can connect with the masses. Isn't that what you want...*your message to be heard?*

Have you ever asked yourself, "How did *this* guest, or *that* expert, get on TV?" What you will learn in this book is what I do as a television producer, and what producers like me do. You will get a full understanding of the behind-the-scenes thinking. Once you get into the mind of a television producer, you will begin to believe, "Hey, I can do that on TV too!" That is why it is a good thing that you are reading this today.

There are no accidents. I have booked many people in situations that seem just like accidents. One time, while producing on the *Donny & Marie* show, we booked television host Greg Proops for an appearance. He hosted *Rendez-view* and is a regular on *Whose Line Is It Anyway?* He's a very funny guy. We decided to do an extra segment with him, and we were looking for an activity. A former production assistant that I had worked with at the now off-the-air WBIS-TV in NYC produced what I thought was such a fun show called *Karaoke Cabaret* for VH1. I thought a similar smaller version of this idea would be fun to produce on the *Donny & Marie* show.

We had a day to cast and produce this six-minute segment. We asked the show band to audition a few folks from the audience who liked to sing or dreamed of being a singer. I called an executive assistant from TV-G (a horse-racing network) and asked her if she wanted to participate, because I had heard her sing one night at a karaoke bar. To my delight, she accepted.

As the day went on, I knew that, to round off my cast of four karaoke singers, I would need an older man to sing a fun song. In my fantasy, I hoped that the last person would be a Harry Belafonte type singing the

"Day-O" song. How fun would that be for a segment with Greg Proops? Then, a producer who was a colleague of mine went out to lunch. Upon his return, he said, "You're not going to believe this, but there is a man standing on the corner by Trader Joe's and the Sony complex, with a big boat on his head with a sign that reads, 'Put me on TV.'"

We booked him on the show and he sang the "Day-O" song as Greg Proops emceed the *Donny & Marie* karaoke cabaret. *Yes, that is a true story!*

> In my seminars I always say, "If we don't need you today, tomorrow, or this year, we may need you next year, next show…now." And that is the truth too.

Just this morning, I received an email stating that a local show (with just *one* television producer) is looking for someone who lost a lot of weight on his or her own diet plan to talk about the personal success and struggle.

I also received a phone call yesterday from a manager who said that *Soap Talk* was looking for a self-defense expert for a taping this Sunday. Hers was out of town; did I know anyone? Are *you* one? Are you available this Sunday?

The network of producers is finite. We all know, help, and support one another find the guests and stories that we need. We move around a lot from show to show. Our Rolodexes become our most valuable asset.

Your job is to connect with these ever-moving, ever-changing television producers and become a professional television guest or expert—aka *TV guestpert*—and get your product or idea on TV. Like a good martini that is shaken, not stirred, there is a science to this skill, a patience to the sell with a twist of serendipity.

Chapter 1
Behind the Scenes of TV

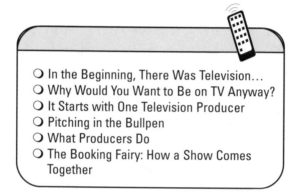

In the Beginning, There Was Television…

Television is a very young industry.

Ten years ago, there was no TiVo.

Thirty years ago, mention cable TV or HBO and you'd get "Say what?" in response.

Fifty years ago, a color TV was something many middle-class families could not afford.

Seventy years ago, the very idea of television seemed like science fiction to the average person. One might as well talk about putting men on the moon…

There are senior citizens who remember life as it was before the advent of television. Their children grew up with TV as a window on the world, glimpsing history-making images such as Elvis on Ed Sullivan, the famous Nixon-Kennedy debate, daily tragedy in Vietnam, Martin Luther King Jr.

marching for civil rights, and, most miraculously, a man setting foot on the moon itself. Now our most recent generation is growing up with prenatal "TV" images of themselves tacked to the fridge of excited expectant parents!

Television's accessibility factor has been radically altered since its initial 1950s boom. Most important for our purposes here, the very face of television has changed in recent decades. Once costly technology is now available for home usage. Anybody with a camcorder and a home computer can make a movie, documentary, or "TV show" of their own.

Once the domain of the few, television is now open to literally *anybody* with an interesting story to tell. Now more than ever, television is made up of faces of everyman. It has become every person's birthright to experience his or her fifteen minutes of fame on television.

Do you know what this means for you? That learning the skills to get on TV is a necessity for modern-day living. What used to be a random accident, being discovered is an essential part of life today, and if you master the skills to get on TV, you can elevate yourself, your career, and your hopes and dreams to an accessible level never before imagined. And it begins with understanding the television terrain and how to negotiate the business that impacts every part of your life, whether you are aware of it or not.

Why Would You Want to Be on TV Anyway?

I can't answer that for you, but I can tell you what television can do for you! It can raise your profile. It's a vehicle for telling your story, your message. It can reach millions. The publicity is worth millions of dollars if you know how to position yourself. Almost all TV hosts were TV guests first! It can bring attention to a cause, a charity, a company, a consciousness. It can give you access to other worlds, people, economic classes, and status. It's a reflection of our selves, our lives, and our society. And the ability to make it work for you is written on these pages.

It's easy to take TV for granted. It's the background music of our lives. Newscasts and talk shows chatter on as we wake in the morning, get ready for work, eat dinner, and prepare for bedtime.

And it's true: much of what's on the box is not really worth our undivided attention. There's too much noise and not enough useful signal. This is precisely what makes us forget sometimes that TV is such a powerful and transformative informational medium.

In the blink of an eye, in the click of a remote—one story, one cause, one fact can be broadcast to millions of viewers across the nation. Sometimes, it is just pet rocks or a new diet; it's OK to have fun, after all! But as often as not, we can be exposed to stories of real value that enrich our lives by making us feel more involved with and connected to life.

It Starts with One Television Producer

It's not the relationship with the show or the show's audience that should be cultivated first when attempting to get on TV. To bridge the gap between the two worlds, the world where you desire to get on TV and the world where you actually get there, you must get in contact with a producer. The following story is one example of how connecting with the television producer can change the course of a life.

This was the case with Jackie Johnson, a woman who suffered from agoraphobia (the fear of leaving one's own home) for twelve long years. What motivated her to overcome this paralyzing illness? Jackie had not only an important story to tell, but she needed help to do it. Telling her troubling story to her neighbors or via newspaper or radio programs was not enough. It took the power of the television medium to provide Jackie Johnson with a platform to tell her story and ruffle some feathers. It was television that changed her reality and helped her chase her daughter's suspected murderer.

I had just come back from a celebrity bingo fundraiser at the Ramada Plaza Hotel in West Hollywood. The event was designed to raise money for Jackie Johnson's legal fund. NBC's highly rated and much celebrated *Dateline* was there. After years spent building momentum, Jackie's story was about to hit the big leagues and garner national media exposure with the widest possible audience.

Jackie Johnson's story goes like this: in the spring of 2001, her twenty-one-year-old daughter, Erin, was vacationing in Cabo San Lucas, Mexico, with her boyfriend. She had agreed to a last-ditch effort to patch up their faltering relationship. Days later, Erin's lifeless body was discovered on a lonely beach. She had been strangled. All evidence clearly pointed to her boyfriend as the prime suspect. The Mexican authorities arrested him, but soon afterward, he was released without charge and allowed to return to the United States.

According to the law, in an unsolved murder, unless Mexico asks the United States for help with the investigation, the boyfriend, a suspect and a U.S. citizen, will remain a free man. Jackie Johnson, just another mother in Michigan, was powerless against the multitude of political, cultural, and economic differences, and the legal system of another country.

Sadly, such unresolved murder cases are not uncommon—look at the headlines of the teenager vacationing in Aruba. How did one brave and grieving mother compel the vast bureaucracy of U.S. law enforcement to take notice of the injustice at hand here? Her only weapon available was television.

Let's flash forward in time to the bingo fundraiser at the Ramada. By enlisting *Dateline* to be at the event, they turned the spotlight on a case that otherwise might have remained in relative obscurity, a story that may never have gone beyond local and regional news markets.

Dateline will air this story as a full one-hour exclusive segment. Jackie hopes that, after the show airs, Mexican authorities will be forced to concede to a proper investigation about the death of Jackie Johnson's daughter, Erin. They will have no choice but to enlist the help of the United States government and the FBI in locating Erin's boyfriend and to have him extradited back to Mexico to face charges.

You couldn't pay for publicity like this. It's powerful and develops its own momentum. And Jackie got the ball rolling without the benefit of a public relations agent. Such is the power of grassroots, do-it-yourself publicity. You see, Jackie Johnson's journey to the national stage began with one single television producer.

You only have to grab the attention of one single television producer to get on TV! And I'm going to show you how. But first, before we reveal the rest of Jackie Johnson's story, and how *Dateline* got involved, it's time to meet the producers...

Pitching in the Bullpen

So where does the process start? It's Monday morning and across the nation production teams gather in nondescript, often open office spaces known as the bullpen. There are TV shows to produce, stories to develop, guests to book, and audiences to entertain and edify. Tempus fugit—time flies!

> ### *BULLPEN*
>
> The open office space in which a show's staff works, shouts, and books shows.

The pitch meeting is when the creative staff members gather with their newspaper and magazine clippings from the weekend to pitch a dozen or so show ideas. Some are accepted. Many are not. It's a competitive environment. Each staff member wants to get his or her show concepts into production with management's approval. Time is always of the essence. Everybody is looking for an edge. The process is not studied and measured, at least not at this stage; here it is dynamic and fluid. Ideas are pitched, modified, and accepted or rejected with rapidity.

Let's bring your point of view into this scenario. What are these people pitching and discussing? *Your stories!* Your ideas, your profession, your personality, your life experience: in short, *you*. You may even be pitched without your knowledge or consent. I've seen entire stories written about a guest idea with his or her picture tacked to the show board, and then cancelled without the prospect ever knowing. In this book, we are going to empower you to participate in this process to your own advantage!

The staff's reputation is on the line during these pitch meetings, based on how well they can sell you. And although you have no direct control over precisely how they present you, with the right pitch (idea), hook (the irresistible twist that makes your idea a must-see), and platform (the belief your message stands upon), your material will be putting its best foot forward, so to speak. So to rephrase a popular saying: *preparation is nine-tenths of the law.* If a producer can't confidently take your pitch into the room and sell you, you're toast! If you are well prepared and professional, if you do the job of a producer for a producer, it makes it that much easier when he or she "pitches" you in one of those bullpen meetings. Help them put their money where your mouth is.

PLATFORM

A. The core belief upon which your message stands.
B. Your evolving portfolio of print, radio, and television appearances, all of which reinforce your belief and message.
   We'll talk about both aspects of platforms in this book, but they are so closely linked as to almost be the same thing, because belief transforms into action. Who you are is amplified by what you do and say.

In later chapters, we'll take a close look at pitches, hooks, and platforms. Getting your idea, story, or product into that all-important staff pitch meeting is another key step we'll cover, because there's no point getting all dressed up if you have no place to go! But for now, just know that this is the process.

What Producers Do

Producing is a demanding, high-pressure job. One of the producer's most important skills is the ability to understand a story's construction and see how that story may or may not fit into his show's format (a show's unique personality profile). This can be like looking for a needle in a haystack or a diamond in a coal mine! Producers need experience and creativity to aid their search for compelling material.

FORMAT

Literally, a show's *form* or *shape*. You can also think of format as a show's personality profile. Some show formats are issue-oriented; others are geared more towards entertainment.

Producers will be able to see multiple angles in any given story, and, if possible, find ways of framing the material that makes it appropriate for their show. A story's content is not changed, but its context, or the way in which it is viewed, can undergo many alterations. For example, in Jackie Johnson's case, the story of her search for justice might be shown as a mother's quest for closure, or as an unsolved mystery, or as a piece about the loopholes in interlocking international justice systems. Same story, different context.

The deadline pressure for a producer in any format is challenging, to say the least. The demand is to move quicker, faster, and cheaper. I have to call people all the time the day before a taping and say, "Can you get on a plane and be here tomorrow for a taping?" The response is always, "If I had more notice…" But I *never* have more notice! It's an "eternal now" situation. Forget yesterday, forget next week, heck, even forget tomorrow, because we may need you *right now*! Be ready to seize any opportunity when and if that phone finally rings for you…

A daytime television show usually has a week or less to turn around a one-hour show from conception to execution. Imagine planning, organizing and cooking a Thanksgiving dinner feast with all the fixings for fifty friends and family…in two days! We work hard for our money.

A show budget can range from five- to six-digit figures. That may sound exorbitant, but trust me, there is no caviar or massage therapist to be found on the balance sheets. A program like *The Tony Danza Show,* for example, with a musical band, can cost $100,000 to $150,000 per episode to produce. That is a lot of money for producers (usually in their late twenties) to be responsible for, and we are solely accountable for everything on the show, including you!

Then there is an entire production crew, often numbering up to fifty highly skilled professionals, to be paid, plus expensive equipment rentals, catering, and so on. We producers are also responsible for clearing the rights to any songs we may make use of on the show. Even showing a shot of the Hollywood sign costs money and requires permission to use. Heck, every word and phrase that you read on screen is devised by us, the producers.

So a show's producers really are responsible for *everything* that comes out on the TV screen (Color schemes: yes! Guests' outfits: yes! Making sure you get made up perfectly: yes!)

Gather round, folks, because I'm about to share a secret with you. Here it is: Ultimately, a show is only as good as the guests that appear on it, and a producer is only as good as his or her last show. All that we do would be for naught if you, the television guests of America (and beyond), were not so darned fascinating, entertaining, riveting, funny, charming, soulful...

Remember: We, the television producers of America, need YOU!

Producers' responsibilities include the following:

- Flushing out the show or segment ideas
- Researching the topic
- Booking the guests
- Producing the beginning, middle and end of the show or segment
- Writing the scripts
- Briefing the hosts
- Selecting music, props, wardrobe
- Acquiring clearance permission and rights
- Staying within budget
- Executing the idea on the show
- Making sure the intention of the idea makes it to the television screen

You and I are coming together for a reason. I have *never* not delivered a show. I have *never* been assigned a show from a boss, a studio, a network and told him or her, "You know, I really can't do that. I can't find such a person." As a producer, I must make it happen. Somehow, we do! That's why I'm still working. Again, I'm just making the point that we are always looking for people like you! My viability as a producer is based on the strength of my Rolodex with your name in it!

Of course, you need to make being found as easy as possible for me (which is why you are reading this book), but we producers sometimes have to shake the trees and look behind the couch to find what we're seeking. Meet me halfway and you'll get on TV.

The Booking Fairy: How a Show Comes Together

You think I'm joking, don't you? But there is such a thing as the Booking Fairy out there. Believe me, I've lain on the floor of my office, wailing "My show tapes in twenty-four hours and I need somebody somewhere to donate a free house!" Then the phone will ring and everything will fall into place. Of course, I may have torn out a handful of hair while waiting for the Booking Fairy to sprinkle her magic serendipity dust, but in the end, it's worth all the aggravation. It's all about making the best show possible.

Back when I produced for *The Maury Povich Show,* I was assigned the "Wishes and Dreams" episode, in which six guests would have a wish granted. My producing team (team = me and my associate producer) had a five-day lead time in which to prepare this program from scratch, as there were other *Maury* episodes, some of them scheduled to tape on the very same day, in simultaneous development. Imagine taking your high school SATs on the same day as the prom *and* the student body presidential election. A full plate indeed!

The "Wishes and Dreams" show was to be divided up into six guest segments for a total of forty-six minutes of running time: commercials account for the other fourteen minutes. Each segment had to play like a mini-show. Every guest had to be introduced and interviewed, the wishes and dreams had to be set up and delivered upon, then we had to wind the guest's story down go to a commercial break with a flashy stay-tuned come-back and do it five more times.

From A to Z

It's Thursday morning. The "Wishes and Dreams" show tapes Tuesday morning. At seven a.m., my associate producer (AP) and I go "dream hunting" as we begin putting out feelers to our producer contacts to see if they know of any good "dreams come true" candidates. Then the Rolodex—a producer's magic mirror, believe me!—is again consulted for memorable or familiar guest experts who may be able to find a client or a lead for potential ideas. (The payback in this is that the professional TV guest or expert—aka TV guestpert—gets to appear on the show along with the story they helped us find and nurture.) In this way, we hope to "back into" a Wishes and Dreams story, and find a candidate via our network of connections. This backing-in technique is often used by producers. We just need to add you to that list.

My AP and I have now come to the limits of the map and our Rolodexes. From here on out, we're in *terra incognita,* unknown territory. This is where a great many of the best guests and stories come from. If you follow the lessons in the book and diligently build your platform, this is where you will be lurking, like a tiger hidden in the grass. We producers always take the next step, hoping to pounce on a fresh story or individual, but we don't mind getting pounced upon either. Surprise us!

We now scour the Internet, blogs, newspapers from *USA Today* to small-scale regional periodicals, listen to hotline phone messages to the show, and simultaneously sift through the voluminous viewer mail suggestions and requests. We draw up a list of potential guests and get busy.

Next we send out FedEx packages containing letters of inquiry. We track down individuals mentioned in newspapers and magazines. We make phone calls to potential guests who did give us their numbers (lots of people fail to include their phone numbers when they send in letters, or their email addresses have been discontinued). We contact organizations if I have a creative idea to do a surprise for a type of story I am looking for.

In these ways, we chase down "bad stories" that initially seemed interesting but now fail to make the grade. Maybe a phone number has changed, or somebody has moved out of town, or a person is a poor speaker, or a story just plain turns out to be false or exaggerated.

Reasons Potential Guests Get Turned Down

- Inarticulate
- Not enthusiastic or passionate
- Uncooperative
- Lacks professionalism
- Inconsistencies in their experience or story

The stories that seem promising get written down on index cards and placed on the office's *show board*. We now have a "map" of one hundred possibilities that have to be whittled down to six guests and stories.

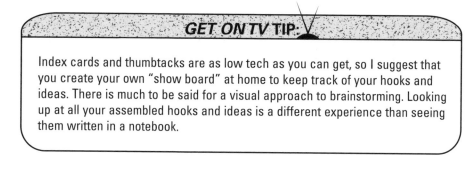

GET ON TV TIP:

Index cards and thumbtacks are as low tech as you can get, so I suggest that you create your own "show board" at home to keep track of your hooks and ideas. There is much to be said for a visual approach to brainstorming. Looking up at all your assembled hooks and ideas is a different experience than seeing them written in a notebook.

We work out and write out possible "surprise" story structures. How would Guest X's segment be designed? Can we figure out a way to surprise the folks who are in on the surprise? Meanwhile, we keep making phone calls. We have informal Q&A sessions with possible guests or the friends and family members who have alerted us to dreams and wishes that might be fulfilled. We're looking for information in a nutshell at this point. And as we narrow down our idea of what dreams and wishes might be suitable for the show, we have to start finding potential gift donors.

We're still at work at eleven o'clock waiting for return phone calls from potential guests who work late or live in different time zones. By the end of day one, we have streamlined the show board. We have a rough idea and outline for the show, but there are still a great many variables and contingencies to be worked through.

Friday rolls around and we're back at work at seven, opening return FedEx packages from the phone-numberless guests. Many packages contain photos of our potentials: alas, we have to eliminate people who are not "TV-friendly." Then we focus on our guest families. Do the adults need travel documents? Will the children require on-set teachers?

Surprises and gifts get firmed up. Which plastic surgeon do we use to grant this dream? Who is going to donate a free house? At this point, you may be asking, "Why do businesses and professionals give away expensive free services?" Well, altruism and generosity are a major factor, but so is national TV exposure...I call this the "unspoken agreement." We'll make sure you have yours in place too for when the phone rings. See chapter 9.

With the available material assembled from FedEx packages, emails, newspaper articles, guest interviews, and photos, we assemble a research package for Maury, as well as a script that lays out the order and structure of the segments. We continue to make the show solid. More phone calls to guests go out, telling them what to expect and how their segments will play out. We make advisory comments on wardrobe, which is not as easy as you might think.

Then it's on to the internal side of show preparation as we meet with the show director for the "Wishes and Dreams" episode, as well as key crew members such as the cameramen and their teams. Sixty crew members need to know their roles in the special episode's organization. We lay out the show's structure and block out which guest emerges from what part of the stage, and how we keep people's identities a secret for as long as possible, if needed. Then we figure out who comes into the building at what time. We can't have a surprise blown if Little Timmy sees his long-lost Uncle Bob, can we?

The weekend arrives and work continues apace. Details continue to evolve, change, and come into focus. These two days are spent locking in the free gifts and donations. Note: by this point on the "Free House" story, I have received *no calls back* at all. I am too busy to get properly panicky.

Before we know it, Monday has arrived bright and early, as Mondays always do. We prep our host as to each and every guest's details, as well as the timing of the surprises. This is a little like having an afternoon's rehearsal for a play that is part scripted and part improvised. Maury is a consummate pro, so this part of our day is peaceful compared to what's just around the corner. Guests have begun to arrive in town and check into hotels. Lost luggage and wrong room reservations must be ironed out. Even the most confident person needs quite a bit of handholding. I'd get stage fright too, with only three-days warning before my very first television appearance!

Now it's Tuesday. Everything is in motion. All the factors and details click into place. The crew sets up in the studio. The guests arrive, then the studio audience. It's showtime, folks, and all I have is one final detail to take care of: I have to ensure that everything goes *perfectly*.

When Things Go Wrong

Let's return to my seemingly doomed bid to land a free house. As you may recall, I am lying on the floor of my office, wailing *"My show tapes in twenty-four hours and I need somebody somewhere to donate a free house!"*

Why did I need a house? In the show's viewer mail file, I had found a wonderful letter from a big-hearted seventh grade girl that touched me deeply. She wrote to Maury about a neighboring family that lived down the street. Their home had burned to the ground. One of the family's twin siblings mistakenly believed her sister was still in the blazing house. Without fear for her own safety, this heroic child rushed back inside. She died from smoke inhalation. To make the situation all the more heartbreaking, her sister had been outside the house the entire time.

We booked the girl who wrote the letter and her mother, but did not tell them how *The Maury Povich Show* was going to respond to their neighbors' crisis. The neighbors were then booked for the very next Tuesday, although the mother was unable to attend: she was still hospitalized with a lung ailment from the fire. And what could we do to make this family's wishes come true without trivializing the tragic loss of their daughter? The usual tricks up our sleeves—clothes, makeovers, or holidays—were not going to be enough. The solution was, in a way, as obvious as it was elegant. *The Maury Povich Show* was going to get them a brand-new home.

Remember the last section with all that crazy detail juggling? Well that all goes down, and as I said then, I canvassed the country, from East Coast to West, searching for contractors who might be willing to donate an entire home for our primary wishes and dreams family. That Thursday, phones rang, messages were left, letters were mailed, and press kits went out detailing our family's crisis. It was a major communications volley, yet the Friday passed without a return serve. Then the weekend came and went and brought no responses either.

I tried Habitat for Humanity, but our request did not mesh with their charity policies. Pre-fab housing drew blanks, as did mobile home outlets. As the days progressed, my anxiety level began to climb. The very possibility of blowing a show segment was bad enough, but it was made all the more pressing by our primary family's real and urgent needs. The as-yet-to-exist free house played much upon my mind, which was also focused on dealing with the thousand other details concerning the five other segments.

On Monday, I crossed the Rubicon. The guests were all en route via airplane. There was no free house, nor even a remote "maybe" on the horizon. Even Maury was occasionally looking at me askance, as if to say, "A house? For real?"

Tuesday morning at nine a.m., with taping set to begin at eleven, the Booking Fairy finally came through. *The phone rang.* A pre-fab contractor in Oregon promised to give our family a *free home* worth ninety thousand dollars. We had found our benefactor and fairy godmother (the Booking Fairy's third cousin). We had secured a gift that would make the "Wishes and Dreams" show truly special, for the participating family, our staff, and the viewing audience. In the end, the show was a success, and a small, warm ray of hope shone upon the grieving family.

You may recall that *Oprah* opened its 2004 season by giving away a Pontiac to each member of the studio audience. Soon after that, they taped a Christmas show during which they presented a studio audience of three hundred schoolteachers with watches, laptop computers, spa trips, flat screen TVs, and even a washer and dryer. Each teacher received *all* of those gifts (and more!). But while this looks like a smooth and effortless publicity stunt, you can be sure that somewhere behind the scenes, there was some producer working the phones, making the deals, and hoping that the Booking Fairy would appear and magically find gift-giving sponsors appropriate to the teacher-friendly audience.

Maybe there's a television producer out there at this very moment, frantically looking for somebody with your type of expertise or experience. But more often than not, there may be a plethora of individuals with a similar skill set or tale to tell. Don't count on the Booking Fairy to hook you up! You need to maximize your potential visibility and carefully target the relevant member of a TV show's producing staff.

Recapping, to get on TV, start with grabbing the attention of just one television producer. The fallacy of many TV guest hopefuls is that they make the show or the show's audience the focus of their attention and efforts; but it's the busy, often frantic, television producer who is your first audience.

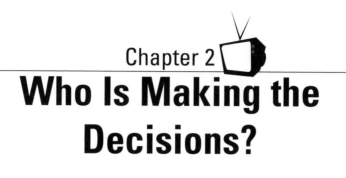

Chapter 2

Who Is Making the Decisions?

IN THIS CHAPTER:

- The Hierarchy of a Television Show
- Variations in Producer Titles
- Jackie Johnson's Story…Continued

Who makes the decisions in television? That's easy: everybody. Decisions are made every minute of the day. Even a receptionist can make a decision by returning your call or making your message a priority or not.

But obviously, not everybody carries equal weight. So, you may be wondering, whom do I contact? Who is my target? Can there be multiple targets? In terms of finding these answers, take a look at the hierarchy of a television show.

The Hierarchy of a Television Show

1. Studio or network
2. Executive overseeing programming or development
3. Executive producer
4. Supervising producer
5. Show producer
6. Segment producer or associate producer

7. Booker or researcher

8. Production assistant

9. Intern

Who on this list has the most power when you pitch your product, self, or idea on TV? You'd be amazed...the intern can have as much power as the studio head! Say what? Why?

The Intern

Interns are usually younger, and they tend to have their finger on the pulse of societal and pop culture trends. They go out to clubs and concerts and are closer to "what's coming up" and what's hip. Senior staff members listen closely to what interns have to say. And at the intern stage, it's easier to gain access to interns than producers.

NEWS FLASH

You have *more* opportunities than just trying to get to the top producer. Your job is just to get *in*. Once you are in the loop, a good idea counts, no matter who is taking it in to the pitch meeting.

Don't underestimate interns, as they are tomorrow's producers and studio heads. They are the fundamental support staff in television. They open mail, answer phones, do research, run errands, and overhear most of the office gossip. They know which producer is looking for what topics, and which staff members might be more receptive to a left-of-field pitch. A good intern wants to get a job, so they act as if they actually already *have* a job. An intern who can pitch a good idea or come to the rescue with a great guest becomes a recognized intern among the faceless, nameless others.

OF INTERNS AND MOGULS

Nineteenth-century author Horatio Alger Jr. wrote scores of best-selling short novels about plucky young down-and-out kids who attained the American Dream of success and wealth via hard work and determination. In the twentieth century, mega-moguls like David Geffen started their careers in the mailrooms of various talent or record industry companies.

The Production Assistants

The entry-level paid positions on a show's staff are production assistants. They perform the same jobs as the interns, but are relied upon more heavily. In addition, on some shows, production assistants are involved in creating content and ideas. This is significant because they are required to come to the table with an understanding of the show and what is involved, as well as with new ideas and faces.

The Researcher

A researcher is like the show's private detective. Using the telephone and Internet search engines, they scour the information grid in search of guest candidates, as well as new leads to fresh topics and individuals. Can you be found with ease? Do you have a website? Ask yourself: How would a researcher find out about me? This chapter will help you plan a strategy to maximize your accessibility profile.

GET ON TV TIP:

Get wired! There's no real excuse anymore not to have a website: they are affordable, easy to design, and vital to establishing an easily accessed media profile.

Sometimes showing is better than telling!

The Booker

The booker takes up where the researcher leaves off. Once we've found potential guests, we have to check them out. Bookers put out phone calls. What does your answering machine message or voice mail greeting say about you? Do you respond promptly to your phone messages? Is there more than one number at which to reach you?

A booker reports to the producing team about the viability of their content agenda: which guest candidates have the edge? Who is a character, who is persuasive, who is hesitant?

A producer may, for example, assign a booker to find him an expert who overcame shyness to talk about a new study on shyness for the five-o'clock news. Or, perhaps a story is missing a point of view, and in order to produce a balanced segment, a specific type of pundit or expert may be required. When I was supervising a pilot for Telepictures, a division of Warner Brothers Studios, we were producing a segment about the hotly debated issue of pilots possessing handguns for protection while on the job. We booked a female pilot who supported the idea, a flight attendant who opposed it, and to balance it out, we had the booker find us a personal story. She located a family member who'd lost a relative in one of the hijacked 9/11 flights. Had this plane's pilots been carrying firearms, the tragic outcome may well have been different. We felt this personal point of view was essential to tell in order to shape the segment.

Bookers have to have nerves of steel. They talk on the phone all day long. Think of them as the all-knowing switchboard operators that may connect you to the show you want to be on.

The Associate Producer

Associate producers act in a booking capacity too. They are literally "content finders." Think of them as circus ringmasters tasked with pulling together a great show. When the orders come down the ranks to book a story on X, Y, or Z, it's the associate producers who are fundamentally responsible for making the bookings happen. The associate producers pull the biggest workload in terms of research and bookings. They are usually the first to make contact with a TV guestpert candidate. They are the producing eyes and ears that filter material and ideas up the chain, and the APs are the ones doing the legwork for the ideas that come down the chain. APs are an essential target when making contact with a show.

The Casting Department

Question: What do you call a passel of bookers? Answer: A casting department or agency. Daytime television talk shows don't have casting departments. Casting departments or agencies search for candidates for reality TV shows, a topic we'll cover later. Casting agencies also find acting talent for TV dramas and sitcoms, but this part of their job description falls outside of our specific goals of getting booked on "nonfiction"—aka "scripted"—programs.

The Producer

The show producers or segment producers oversee the bookings, pull all the content together, and create the segment or show. They have to sell a show concept or topic to their superiors. They write the show's script and carefully shape each segment so an episode has a structured beginning, middle, and end. It is the producer who ultimately chooses whether or not to put his or her neck out for a guest whom other staff members have located, vetted, and approved. Think of producers as field commanders: they're down in the trenches, marshalling the troops and making sure content and format orders from up top are carried out efficiently.

SEGMENT PRODUCER

A position in between associate producer and producer.

The Supervising Producer

Senior or supervising producers, and sometimes coordinating producers, are responsible for overseeing the crafting of shows and segments. They are directly involved in developing the material, but not necessarily in a hands-on manner.

The Executive Producer

The executive producer oversees a show's day-to-day operations and ensures that the program's overall stylistic vision and format are being well maintained. EPs are busy in all ends of production, including planning upcoming content, keeping close tabs on postproduction (editing), and delivering progress reports to the studio executives who represent a given show's owners. Even though they are the top decision-makers in a show's structure, they are not directly involved with booking. Like the supervising producer, if they see a pitch in which they are interested, they usually pass it down to the producer, segment producer, or associate producer to evaluate. When I've held these positions, I usually delegate responsibility to junior producers. For example, I may come across a guest and pass his or her info on to a segment producer, who then determines if the guest is viable or not. You might attract my attention directly through your own actions, but if you fail to win over my staff, I won't question their judgment.

The Studio Executives

The studio executives represent the business body that is paying for the programming and, by extension, that body's stockholders. They are guardians of the bottom line creatively (good show = good ratings) and financially (good ratings = profits). They contribute to a show's content on occasion, but are not necessarily involved in the pitching process as are producers. After pitches have been accepted internally, the executive producer usually goes over these ideas with the studio executive to see if they match the overall vision of the show.

Studios or Networks

Studios or networks purchase a quantified order of shows that fit into their programming schedule and match the branding of their company.

Even if you live across the street from a network affiliate, don't bother trying to pitch there: that's where all the boring business and paperwork gets done!

As you can see, it's quite a layered hierarchical infrastructure. And this doesn't take into account the complex internal politics within a show's staffing structure. It's a challenging structure to penetrate, but it can be done. You can do it.

But Wait! What about the Hosts?

While hosts are the all-important public face of a show, and therefore a primary branding feature, they are not directly involved in the internal development process. The job of the hosts is to execute the content of the show to perfection. Think of them as the face of the product.

Given the volume of material that a host is expected to learn, know, understand, and present, it's not physically possible for them to be involved with the details of the bookings or to attend every pitch meeting. For that matter, it's simply not their job. They have to be ready, prepared, and great when it counts, and that is on camera. Of course, the host's input is valued, and they do have "right of refusal," but if they receive a pitch, they usually pass it on to the producing staff. Therefore, pitching to the host is not an effective way of getting your product or idea on television.

One exception that comes to mind is television reporters. They take a more active role in producing their segments and yet, like hosts, they *are* considered on-air talent.

Variations in Producer Titles

There are three types of producers:
1. Producers who create content
2. Producers who manage money
3. Producers who sell programming

Attention! You must focus your attention *only* on producers who create content. Other producers manage money (no, don't ask them for spare change!), and there are also producers who pitch and sell programming to studios and networks.

There are potentially confusing variations in producer's titles. Many titles are interchangeable or even vary from show to show. For example, in news, a line producer calls the show from the production booth (command central) during a taped or live broadcast. But in Los Angeles, a line producer solely manages a show's budget. Coordinating producers' roles vary, with some managing content and some money. Blessed are the bean counters...but you don't need to contact them!

When in doubt over some obscure producing prefix, keep this simple rule in mind: always aim for *content producers.*

So, to sum it up, the middle range is where you should target your pitch: researchers, bookers, associate producers, segment producers and producers. They are the core group that are working the phones and searching the web. They are the people reading the newspaper articles and ripping out the headlines for their shows. They choose every element that goes into their product: the show itself.

Jackie Johnson's Story...Continued

I said we'd be coming back to Jackie, didn't I? But first, let's backtrack and see what lead to that fateful bingo fundraiser at which *Dateline* was present.

In 2001, I was working as a supervising producer on a show called *Talk or Walk* for Tribune Entertainment. Joe Scott, one of the associate producers under my supervision, was making regular use of a service called IRD (Industry Research and Development), which searches out topics and news slugs from across the country.

SLUG

An abbreviated title that describes a topic. Example: *Woman Gives Birth to Quintuplets.*

Joe was drawn to one particular slug—"Woman Needs Closure on Daughter's Death." It brought him back to a time when he'd been in a serious car accident and his own mother told him, "I don't know what I would do if I lost you." Joe felt a personal connection to the story, what I call a "producer's heart," and thus tracked down Jackie Johnson with the intention of possibly pitching her as a segment on the show.

After fully researching news articles relating to Erin's murder and Jackie's quest, Joe presented this story in *Talk or Walk's* morning pitch meeting. He created a pitch with a hook that fit into the show format. Joe also had to paint a clear and compelling picture as to how he would translate this woman's story for television.

Talk or Walk's format was as follows. Each segment would feature two guests who had some sort of prior disagreement. They come on the show, hash things out with the aid of the host, and if the heat gets too high, they can literally talk or walk away.

Initially, and surprisingly, Joe set up a televised confrontation between Jackie Johnson and Erin's boyfriend, the would-be prime suspect. Yeah, I know, that just seems too good to be true, doesn't it? Well of course it fell through. The boyfriend kept hedging his bets and cancelled as the planned tape date approached.

Ordinarily, this might have spelled the end for Jackie and any show other than *TOW*. But recall that Joe had that deep personal connection to Jackie's story. Helping Jackie bring her story to the media was not just a matter of staying in contact with a great guest or doing the right thing for the sake of justice. Joe's heart was invested in Jackie's quest, and his "producer's instinct" knew it would be a phenomenal story for the show's audience. His determination was bolstered by this exceptional mother's unwavering resolve. Erin would get her day in court. Her case would get a thorough hearing.

Joe then arranged for a friend of Jackie's to be a guest on *TOW*. This woman would "walk" from their friendship if Jackie did not back off on her "obsessive" crusade to get to the bottom of her daughter's murder.

Letting go of Erin was a means for Jackie to move on, or so the woman's point-of-view went. She did have a point: Jackie still rarely left her house. Her life had become unhealthy in addition to unhappy.

Alas, there were still more bumps on the road to getting Jackie's story out there. She and her friend were booked for a September 11, 2001, taping. After the attacks on New York and Washington, DC, all air travel was grounded for days. Joe kept Jackie company and soothed her as best as he could. This was a woman who feared leaving her own home, and here she was in the middle of the worst and most unsettling disaster ever to occur on U.S. soil. The segment finally taped on the thirteenth. Jackie cried like a baby as she recounted what had happened to Erin, and what had happened to her own life after this shattering loss.

After *Talk or Walk* was cancelled, Joe stayed in touch with Jackie. And, after her first and only television appearance on *Talk or Walk,* Joe made it his personal mission to harness his skills as a media-savvy producer in the service of Jackie Johnson's crusade for justice on behalf of her daughter, Erin.

"Nobody at all wanted to hear about her story when I began to pitch it," recalls Joe, "because of what had just happened in the world." After September 11, nobody's attention was focused on this type of small-scale story. "Even though I thought it was a compelling story, the rest of the world didn't want to hear it, and understandably so."

"Patience really mattered, and by January and February of 2002, viewers were ready to listen to a different type of story and the door cracked open a little bit." It took about four months from the time Jackie Johnson appeared on *Talk or Walk* to get her booked on the *Sally Jesse Raphael* show, then in its final season.

Joe recounts, "I thought it was the biggest booking ever! My contact at *Oprah* recommended that I try and get her on *Sally.* Then on Monday, the day before Jackie was supposed to fly out, they cancelled her. I thought, *I can't do this anymore—another cancellation, thinking about the near-cancel at* Talk or Walk. Jackie was hysterical with disappointment. It meant the world to her, but the show was in a different space. I never found out why she was cancelled, and I stopped asking."

Did Joe call it quits? Hardly. He redoubled his efforts, which is an important lesson for all of you. This book will help you on the path to Get on TV, but you very well may face a long uphill battle to gain initial exposure and media momentum.

The thing to take away with you here is: *be persistent.* A corollary rule: *Do not take rejection or cancellation personally.* We'll deal with these issues in chapter 9. But really, these rules have universal application, don't they?

Let's get back to Joe, who is right in the thick of things. Jackie's quest is about to gain the crucial momentum that would eventually lead to attention from *Dateline…*

The courage to find her daughter's murderer became one of the hooks that Joe used to pitch Jackie Johnson because Jackie had been an agoraphobic—afraid to leave her own house for twelve years—up until her daughter's death. This woman, who suffered from this debilitating disease, *walked across the United States* to demonstrate her commitment to bringing her daughter's murderer to justice. This publicity stunt transformed a murder story into a personal crusade, and made it stand out a mile from any other similar story.

Joe then shifted his tactics by using the news hook that Mexico's district attorney planned to reopen Erin's case a year after it had been dropped. This was enough of a hook to get Jackie booked on *The View,* and subsequently, on *The O'Reilly Factor.* Both shows have powerful and uniquely different audiences.

Never one to rest on his laurels, especially not in this most personal of cases, Joe designed a third hook: *Could a murderer be living in your hometown?* This masterful new angle made Jackie's story appealing to local news shows. Joe sent out this pitch as a one-sheet (literally, the story described in a single page), which we will discuss in chapter 5. Here we have a perfect example of changing a story's context but not its content. Needless to say, as a producer himself, Joe knew exactly who to target in any given media outlet's hierarchy.

"The biggest challenge that I had in pitching Jackie Johnson was that I was told that I was pitching two separate stories. My question was 'Which part of the story should I tell—the one about the agoraphobic mother who left her home to find her daughter's murderer, or the one about a murder suspect living in your hometown?'" Joe goes on to say, "In fact, in the beginning the story was rejected by the bigger news organizations because they didn't feel that it had an ending. Also, I had the challenge of keeping the details neat and concise. Can you imagine doing that for an unsolved murder story?"

This now brings us full circle to the bingo fundraiser. With media attention behind Joe and Jackie, an effective show reel of her appearances thus far, and a neatly assembled press kit, Joe then arranged a celebrity bingo fundraiser in Los Angeles. The monies raised would go towards defraying expenses needed to pay for a Mexican legal team that would help with Erin's case from the other side of the border. And here, finally, *Dateline* steps into the picture. Its producers determined that Jackie's quest to reopen Erin's murder investigation had more than enough angles and hooks to make for compelling television. So compelling, in fact, that they will devote an *entire one-hour show* to Jackie's story.

Jackie Johnson will never get Erin back: that is something we all know. But Erin will have one great shot at receiving justice, thanks to her heroic, brave, and resolute mother. Jackie's determination and bravery in the face of incredible obstacles took the story, step by step, onto the national media stage and made it her most powerful and truly accessible weapon. And all it took was turning the head of one television producer...

Chapter 3
Pitches, Hooks, and Branding: Who Are You?

IN THIS CHAPTER:

- Tough Love
- Put a Hook on Your Pitch
- Creating a Hook That Grabs a Producer's Attention!
- What's Your Topic?
- How Hooks Do a Producer's Job for Them
- Mission Statement and Credibility
- Summing It Up

Tough Love

It's time for some tough love, folks. We all know honesty is the best policy. Are you ready?

Here it is: *Your pitch isn't good enough.* Breathe deeply, settle down, and let's tackle this problem.

That's right: your pitch isn't good enough...on its own. You need—no, you absolutely *require*—a strong and compelling hook or angle that sells your idea by taking it one step beyond to the next level. It's no good attracting attention from a potential "buyer" if you don't close the deal, is it?

HOOK

A hook is the twist that is applied to your pitch.
For example: *Extreme Makeover Home Edition* is a twist on *Extreme Makeover*. The pitch? *The show that gives your home a face-lift.*

Think of your pitch as a form of talent. Unless we're talking about exceptional genius like Mozart, talent always needs development to become truly noteworthy. A talent for music, math, or cooking will remain a general aptitude without careful nurturing. Practice, we all know, makes perfect.

Your pitch is no different. Your charisma, your brilliance, your unique skill or ability is not enough to guarantee you access to television audiences. Even if you are a doctor, a lawyer, or a mortician, television, no matter how serious a given show or segment, is *show business*. As one very wise media mogul said, "It's not *show show*." Even presidents and their cabinet members have to master the basic principles of performance. All the world's, as William Shakespeare wrote, a stage...

So no matter how compelling your pitch is, you simply have to develop a strong hook that will enable you to attract the interest of producers time and time again. And not just one hook. No sir. Television shows change focus along with the seasons. They roll with current events and trends. You need hooks for all manner of "weather," from rain to snow to shine.

Put a Hook on Your Pitch

I heard a great hook on the evening news: *Marriage makes you fat.* Forget about French fries and éclairs, marriage is the reason you're fat! Now this is a perfect example of a hook. It's the kind of claim that'll make you stop reading that newspaper and pay attention to the TV.

Let's take a step back and take in the larger picture. What is this particular hook selling? What's the most likely pitch behind this catchy angle?

Dieting. Dieting?! Sounds like a bit of a letdown on its own, doesn't it? Imagine if the TV announcer had said—"And next up, another new dieting plan!" This wouldn't garner much interest as there are new diets every week, it seems. If you are writing a diet book, destined to be one of the ten-thousand-plus titles currently listed on Amazon.com, you'd better project something *juicy* that makes you stand out from the pack so that you can be the desired flavor of the month. Hence the hook on the dieting pitch: *Marriage makes you fat.*

This particular hook might in fact tie into a more interesting pitch than dieting, such as the issues of relationship problems, stress, and comfort eating patterns. Maybe there's a new study out from a noted scientific organization that illuminates one of these areas. But these pitches *still* require hooks to sell themselves in a crowded and bustling media landscape. *Marriage makes you fat* remains a viable hook for any of the above pitches: it still grabs the viewers' attention. In this instance, one cleverly crafted hook works for two very different types of topic pitches.

Creating a Hook That Grabs a Producer's Attention!
Let's get ready to sharpen those hooks and play those angles!

To get booked in a flash, you need a pitch that sells, and to generate a pitch that sells, you need a sharp, catchy hook. Like all techniques we cover in this book, ultimately, this all boils down to *you.*

Your hooks and your angles can change all the time. They can change based on the season, current trends in science or popular culture, or for the specific show you hope to be on soon. So you can have multiple hooks at hand, but they have to be time sensitive and show sensitive.

A hook can be based on the character of your name (e.g., *The Naked Chef*).

In Tom Peters's book *The Brand You 50,* he says that: "Most of us—save Martha Stewart and a handful of others—don't think of ourselves as a 'package.' Mistake! Everybody is a package. (He's a ball of fire. She's a pistol. He's the biggest bore I've ever met.) The trick for 'Brand You' is making sure you control your packaging and the message it sends."

In more recent times, individuals like Oprah, Martha Stewart, and the Olsen twins have developed brand recognition with great success. You know what you are getting (what image they are projecting) by their name alone. So here's an important idea: think of yourself as a brand name. Rich Dad, The Love Doctor, The Fitness Gourmet, Sherlock Bones, to name a few brands.

Now no producer expects to book a guest who is backed by a full product line! But as an aspiring TV guestpert, you can certainly strategize your pitches, hooks, and press kits in chapter 5 as if you wish to project yourself as a unique "brand."

PRESS KIT

Your visual calling card. Your press kit is an informational package that you send out to media outlets. It contains newspaper clippings about you, your bio, an edited reel of your appearances on other shows, photo, and press release.

For example, if you are a psychiatrist specializing in dating, marriage, and sexual issues (your pitch), zero in on one particular angle. Your hook might be: frank and honest advice for teens, like Dr. Drew, co-host of the syndicated radio show *Love Line*. Remember Dr. Ruth, the charming, twinkle-eyed septuagenarian sex therapist who became famous in the late 1980s? The very idea of hearing a little elderly lady talk openly about sexual issues and terms was her all-powerful hook, one that propelled her to television and then publishing fame.

Also, on the subject of sex, successful television guest, Dr. Ava Cadell, sexologist, uses the most brilliant hook for her unique branding simply by coining herself a "sexpert" making her the ideal TV Guestpert!

Creating the appropriate hook gives you an "attractive" and "magnetic" charge. It declares your intention and shows producers *precisely* what you are offering so they know what is being passed on to their viewers. The more focused your brand name, the easier it will be to sell yourself and Get on TV.

Hook Workbook

Here are some very general potential hooks and topics. Where might you fit in?

Seasons
Back to school
Halloween
Thanksgiving
Valentine's Day

History
Sinking of the Titanic
The Anniversary of D-Day
The First Woman Doctor

Current Events
An upcoming movie release
The break-up of a famous couple
The World Series

Statistics
A recent study...
According to...
66 percent of...
Half of...

Personal Story
Meet a woman who overcame (adversity here)...
Hero
Super-mom

OK, here we go. Let's take a topic like cooking and a wannabe guest who is a chef. Here's how to tie a nice-n-catchy hook to the above-listed topics.

Example #1: Seasons
Find out the secret ingredient to making fat-free pumpkin pie for Halloween.

Example #2: History
Discover how Abigail Adams's apple pie recipe is still being used at White House dinners.

Example #3: Current Events
Find out how to recreate the same meal that is being served at the Golden Globes.

Note: Take the calendar out and look at the year ahead. Timeliness is a way to get yourself out there and it allows you to reinvent your hook.

Example #4: Statistics
66 percent of adults think it costs the same amount of money to eat out as it does to buy groceries to cook at home; find out why it's not true.

Example #5: Personal Story
Meet a woman who overcame rare Guillain-Barré syndrome through healthy cooking.

Case Study: The Dog Trainer

My career as a television producer is one facet of what I do. I also package my services as a media consultant and travel the country giving seminars about successful pitching strategies. During one such seminar, I met a woman who wanted to break into television as a guest specializing in dog training, which had long been her profession.

Now, although her drive and ambition were commendable, her pitch was not unique. Not by a long shot. Why would a television producer book her? What specifically about *her* being a dog trainer is she selling?

Was she a former army drill sergeant? No. A daring circus lion tamer? No. Had she been raised in the wild by a pack of golden labs? Hardly! While this woman was presentable and gregarious, she had no angle, no hook, no selling point. If a producer can't latch on to your pitch via a good, sharp hook, then the battle is lost. You will sink like a stone to the bottom of the ocean.

Ironically, the very next day after my encounter with the dog trainer, I received a promotional copy of a book from *another* dog trainer. It was called *How to Make Your Man Behave in 21 Days or Less Using the Secrets of a Professional Dog Trainer* by Karen Salmansohn. Now, this is an excellent and creative way in which to sell yourself as a dog trainer *and* a relationship expert. Talk about a dual-purpose perfect hook!

You take what it is you do and give yourself a hook and angle—a spin. Become your own spin doctor. This pitch can be broken down into two different topics: 1) relationships/dating, and 2) dog training.

SPIN

Spin is a term that gained popularity in the 1980s. In political parlance, spinning is what one does for one's chosen candidate or party when bad news needs to be "spun" with a more positive edge (or your opponent's good news needs taking down a peg with a negative opinion).

A *spin doctor* is a pundit who can spin bad news into good, usually as it happens. A senator caught in bed with an intern? Spin: He was showing her what three-hundred-thread-count sheets were because they were working on legislation for the cotton industry!

What's Your Topic?

Mathematically speaking, given my years in television multiplied by the shows I've participated in researching, booking, producing, or supervising, I've been involved with at least ten-thousand-plus guests making their appearance on television. As a result, I have produced what seems like an infinite amount of topics. Here is a much-abbreviated general list.

What topic category does your idea fall under? The following chart serves two purposes: 1) It reinforces the insatiable appetite that producers have to find TV guestperts under a plethora of topics, and 2) For your work in developing hooks, to see how many different categories of topics that your potential subject falls under and how many ways you can spin your expertise.

- *Abuse:* Those knowledgeable about child, domestic, and elder abuse issues.
- *Achievement and Peak Performance:* Those knowledgeable about overcoming barriers to success.
- *Activists:* Those who work for political and social change.
- *Authors:* From both large and small presses.
- *Aviation:* Those knowledgeable about the field of flying and aviation.
- *Beauty:* Those knowledgeable about the field of makeovers, cosmetics, and personal appearance.
- *Biography:* Those who lead fascinating lives.
- *Business:* Those knowledgeable about the corporate world.
- *Career:* Those knowledgeable about the field of career and workplace excellence.
- *Celebrities:* Television and film celebrities and the people who know them.
- *Children:* Authors and those involved with children and schools.
- *Comic Books:* Those knowledgeable about subjects related to their influence, art, or characters.
- *Communication:* Those knowledgeable about the field of interpersonal or business communications.
- *Crime and Justice:* Experts in the field of crime, police investigation, and law.
- *Culture, Heritage, and Languages:* Those knowledgeable about the field of culture, heritage, and languages.
- *Disasters:* Those involved in coping, preparation, and the aftermath of natural or man-made disasters.

- *Discrimination:* Those knowledgeable about ageism, racism, sexism, and health, religious, and cultural discrimination.
- *Dream Interpretation:* Those knowledgeable about dream interpretation.
- *Education:* Those knowledgeable about education standards, violence in schools, homeschooling, or education privatization.
- *Entertainment:* Those knowledgeable about Hollywood celebrities, television, and film.
- *Etiquette:* Those knowledgeable about personal or business etiquette.
- *Family:* Those knowledgeable about family issues.
- *Food and Cooking:* Those knowledgeable about the food industry or cooking.
- *Government:* Those knowledgeable about taxes, conspiracy theories, cover-ups, and governmental spending issues.
- *Health and Well-Being:* Those knowledgeable about nutrition, diet plans, exercise, disease, and health care insurance.
- *History:* Those knowledgeable about the field of past events and historical facts.
- *Human Rights:* Those involved in human rights issues.
- *Humor:* Performers whose specialty is humor and comedy.
- *Leadership:* Those knowledgeable about leadership skills.
- *Mental Health:* Those knowledgeable about recovering from and dealing with mental illnesses, such as phobias.
- *Money and Investments:* Those knowledgeable about budgeting, investing, and preparing for retirement.
- *Motivation:* Those knowledgeable about the field of motivation and peak performance.
- *Movies and Film:* Those knowledgeable about movies and film.
- *Music:* Those knowledgeable about singers, songwriters, and bands.
- *Negotiation:* Those knowledgeable about the art of negotiation.
- *Organizing:* Those knowledgeable on how to organize and add structure to life.
- *Paranormal and Psychic Phenomena:* Those involved in the field of the

paranormal and psychic phenomena.

- *Parenting:* Those knowledgeable about the issues related to the dynamics and skills needed in parent-child relationships.
- *Photography:* Those knowledgeable about the field of photojournalism and photography.
- *Politics and Elections:* Those knowledgeable about the field of politics and elections.
- *Protection and Safety:* Those knowledgeable about the various methods of protecting yourself and loved ones.
- *Psychology:* Those knowledgeable about the field of psychology.
- *Racial Issues:* Those knowledgeable on the topic of racial issues.
- *Relationships:* Those knowledgeable about marriage, divorce, and familial or interpersonal issues.
- *Relaxation:* Those knowledgeable about relaxation techniques and stress reduction.
- *Religion:* Those involved in the field of religion and theology.
- *Scams:* Those knowledgeable about phishing, email scams, and tele-marketing scams.
- *Science:* Those knowledgeable about science and related subjects.
- *Speakers:* Today's leading experts and speakers.
- *Spirituality:* Those knowledgeable about the field of spirituality.
- *Sports:* Professionals and those involved in the world of sports.
- *Survival:* Those knowledgeable about the field of wilderness and urban survival.
- *Travel:* Those knowledgeable about the topic of travel, for business or pleasure.
- *War, Terrorism, and Homeland Security:* Those involved in security-related issues.
- *Wealth and Wisdom:* Those knowledgeable about the field and dynamics of wealth.
- *Workplace and Jobs:* Those knowledgeable about the dynamics of the workplace, including laws, discrimination, and interpersonal issues.

This list is by no means exhaustive. *Far from it.* It simply illustrates the range and the diversity of guests that a producer needs at his or her disposal at any given time on any given show. Our Rolodexes are our most valuable asset, and our need for you is never-ending!

What topic do you or your ideas fall under? Make a list of all the television *topics* you fall under and create topics of your own. Work these topics into pitches, then practice developing hooks that feel fresh, catchy, and sellable.

Case Study: It's Not Rocket Science...Or Is It?

When I branched out from producing to media-consulting clients, one of my first clients was a woman named Mary Spio. Mary is a highly educated engineer with several patents pending, whose next big project was unusual, to say the least. Mary wanted to start up a *dating magazine!*

I was intrigued but puzzled, so to generate some fresh angles and hooks, I decided to play devil's advocate and challenge Mary's pitch. My questions to her were: "Why would anyone buy a dating magazine from an engineer? And why would we put her on TV for *that?* What would there be to talk about?" For better or worse, we all know the stereotype of the boring, nerdy engineer who uses slide-rules and pocket calculators as fashion accessories.

The all-important hook was right in front of us all the time. It suggested itself when Mary divulged exactly what kind of engineer she was: she literally is a *rocket scientist.* It's true! First one I'd ever met, that's for sure. So our hook incorporated this fact—*Rocket scientist launches dating magazine...because beauty* and *brains can't get a date.* Now, engineering may be dry and dull, but rocket science is sexy and cool. Suddenly, the pitch had a new hook and we were rocketing off into the media stratosphere.

Publishing is a very expensive business in which to launch new products, and Mary's magazine, as of this writing, has taken its strategic time getting off the ground. But here's the important point for our purposes: Mary and her magazine plan received an incredible amount of publicity based on the "rocket scientist/beauty and brains" hook alone. Without even having a tangible product to use as a visual aid, Mary got booked *three times* on NBC's *The Other Half,* then appeared on The Fine Living Network's *Radical Sabbatical,* which led to a segment on *Oprah,* which is the "ka-ching!" of TV appearances. But that's not all. Mary's potential magazine also got a write-up in *Folio,* the magazine industry's prestigious periodical of note. Appearances on mega-market radio programs also ensued. That's an impressive record for someone who did not actually have a product on the market yet. Mary's media journey was triggered by her pitch's irresistible, fresh, and funny hook.

How Hooks Do a Producer's Job for Them

The purpose of creating a hook is to do the producer's job. Without a hook, you are asking or expecting them to do the work for you. Say you pitch yourself to a producer and you have no hook. Yet what you do and how you do it are undeniably remarkable, and a phone interview with a producer you've targeted leaves you buzzing. He hasn't committed to booking you, but he thinks that you're *great.*

But the weeks pass and no booking is forthcoming. Why? Chances are that the producer hasn't figured out what to do with you, or how to fit you on the show—the "reason" for putting you on TV. Maybe the right moment will come along that requires a unique individual like you. Maybe the producer will figure out an angle, a hook that makes you attractive to his show's format.

My friends, those are two *whopping* maybes! Remember our little chat about how talent needs to be developed to become noteworthy? Well here we have a fictitious example of impressive talent that fails to ignite, for our purposes, into a simple booking, one of thousands that happen every year. Why? Because, by failing to think out your own hooks, you are implicitly asking the producers to develop a hook for you. That takes the producer's time, which he doesn't have very much of, because he is usually super-focused on the task directly in front of him: i.e., getting compelling, perfect guests! This producer may really think that you are the greatest invention since the wheel, but by placing your prospects of success in his hands, you are giving up control over your career to somebody who means well, but has many other priorities.

If you haven't worked out your own hooks and you pitch to a producer who does not think that you are wonderful right off the bat, guess what the outcome will be? You won't get booked, and what's worse, you won't register on that producer's radar. You won't make it into that all important Rolodex of potential guests if you don't take responsibility for your *entire* pitch.

Listen well: *carpe diem.* Seize the day. *Make your own hooks.* Market yourself. Present that producer with a great hook that *shows* and *tells* him why you are perfect for his show, and what memorable "take-home message" you can deliver to the audience. The key lesson is: *be prepared.* Don't expect others to do footwork that you can or should be doing.

What to Do When Your Hook Fails

NEWS FLASH

If your hook isn't working for you, change it and try another one. Keep trying. Be creative! Mix and match hook concepts and seasonal topics.

That's right. If your first hook fails, *try again.* Don't just offer a minor cosmetic tweak or change. Come at your pitch from a fresh angle. Try developing outrageous hooks just to get your creative juices flowing (but keep these crazy ones to yourself!). Use your spouse, friends, or family as sounding boards, but keep in mind that their love for you may cause them to hold back on their constructive criticism. All ideas come from imaginative "sparks" and anybody can trigger that one perfect hook into being. But keep things in perspective: try to see how a harried producer might view your pitch if he or she gives it a quick glance. From their perspective, they are hearing and seeing an endless stream of pitches. What your family and friends deem original and exciting, might be tired and old to a show producer who is exposed to idea after idea. Some simple advice: Love your hook, but don't be attached to it.

Here is your hook and booking mantra:

> Be flexible. Be creative. Be prepared.

Case Study: Re-Branding Yourself

Change can be a scary and potentially unsettling phenomenon. Many of us prefer smooth sailing. But by never considering what lies down that other path in life, we miss opportunities for new challenges and fulfillment.

Your career path as a TV guestpert is no exception. Don't avoid change, embrace it. There's nothing that television loves more than the shock of the new, so you should periodically look for ways to rekindle your hooks and pitches with novelty.

Meet Pete Siegel, one of my former media consultant clients. Pete is an in-your-face, dynamic body builder who just also happens to be the country's foremost sports hypnotherapist, and the author of numerous self-help/personal development books. As he says, "Talent knows that it has talent, and if we believe in our talent, we aim to make things happen for ourselves. If not, we seek outside help." This gives you a real sense of who Pete is and how he expresses himself. He is no stranger to motivation and challenge.

Pete could easily remain within the niche he has established for himself, but he wants to broaden his horizons, which he feels are beginning to limit what he is capable of doing. Although he's been booked on *Best Damn Sports Show Period* and ESPN, Pete wants to transition from sports hypnotherapy, a specialized field, into life peak performance for a mainstream audience. He wants to help more people overcome their issues and psychological obstacles to success.

This is a challenging task based on his branding alone: a sports hypnotherapist. It implies that he does only one kind of hypnotherapy. Can a sports hypnotherapist help you quit smoking or make you a more confident person? In a session where we were brainstorming potential hooks, we were thinking about a way to spin what he does to the broader audience that exists outside the popular domains of sports.

Professionally, Pete regularly helps star pro athletes overcome performance slumps. How do we spin this pitch to encompass everybody, not just highly trained athletes? In this case, we needed to create a fresh visual and dramatic presentation of what Pete does. We developed a fun but compelling hook: *Hypnotherapist helps mom overcome stage fright by making her dream come true.* We then pitched this hook specifically to *The Wayne Brady Show,* since Wayne is a well-known singer.

We intended to have Pete hypnotize a mom whose dream was to sing on national TV, yet suffered from stage fright. After a TV session with Pete, she would sing a duet with Wayne Brady on his show. This hook is both entertaining and fun (Can the Mom carry a tune? Can she actually be hypnotized?), as well as potentially moving, for we all love it when somebody's dreams come true, right?

Alas, our carefully crafted exploits did not go according to plan! After expressing initial interest, *The Wayne Brady Show* changed executive producers, and the new EP did not wish to develop Pete's segment. The *James Van Praagh* show (James is a psychic medium) also liked the pitch, but it was cancelled unexpectedly. Then, destiny seemed to come a'calling. The *Oprah* show contacted Pete! Everybody wants to get on *Oprah:* it is the gold standard of television shows, and appearing on it is a guaranteed career booster.

Then one day an aggravated Pete called me, and said, "You know, I got a call back from the *Oprah* producer on Sunday." She told him she couldn't use him this fall as the show was now booked up till spring. So close, and yet so far! Pete couldn't believe his string of luck and was extremely frustrated. I said, "Are you kidding me? That's *great* news." Pete had just received a personal phone call from an *Oprah* producer *on a Sunday.* This is a surefire sign that the producer views him as more than just a face in the crowd.

Pete has just made a wonderful contact. Maybe it'll bear fruit for *Oprah*, or maybe the relationship will pay off if and when the producer moves along to another show. Maybe she'll refer him to a colleague. Pete did not get into the game at that moment, but he has become a notable draft pick. Establishing relationships and contacts will almost always pay off in the end. Think of this stage of your career as the investment stage. Dividends will come later. They sure did for Pete, who has just signed with a deal to be a life coach on a new reality series for VH1, doing exactly what he re-branded himself to do!

Mission Statement and Credibility

Your hook should be congruent with your mission statement. What is a mission statement? This is worth highlighting...

MISSION STATEMENT

This is your company's philosophy on conducting business.

Mission statements generally involve a slogan of some sort. In Atlanta, a long-established jewelry retailer has a great radio slogan that has remained the same for thirty years: "Now *you* have a friend in the diamond business."

If you're an individual, what would your mission statement be?

Mission statements usually contain virtues in their phrases. At Jacquie Jordan, Inc., our phrase is to "Educate, Enlighten, and Entertain."

So if you know who you are (mission statement), what you are selling (pitch), and how to design hooks, then you can spin your branding to fit a television program. But you absolutely have to be able to back up what it is you are selling or spinning.

An example: you're a dentist. Your hook and mission statement is that you are "The dentist to the stars." Are you willing to talk about Warren Beatty's cavities on television? Or Halle Berry's perfectly capped teeth? If you say you can deliver such gossip tidbits, then you *must* follow through. So, if you are the dentist to the stars, but you won't discuss your clients on TV, then there's nothing really to talk about, is there? *Backpedaling and failing to deliver what you have promised will kill your career on TV stone dead.* So don't be a blind date that cancels at the last minute! Your credibility is important. Never make promises that you cannot keep.

Practice Developing Your Hook

Before you run out the door with your hook, stop and ask yourself these three important questions first:

1. How does your pitch sound when it's attached to a news hook?
2. Is your pitch timely or out-of-date?
3. Can you attach any interesting statistics to validate your pitch?

Summing It Up

Who are you? It's fair to say that you are your hook. This hook pulls you out of a crowded ocean of potential television guests, and it also reels in producers.

Hooks give your pitch a timeliness, relevance, a reason, an authority. Without these types of angles, your pitch is just another pitch on a list of topics or you are just another professional in the phone book. A producer has to come up with an angle to do his job, but if you can present the hook or a reason, you have a better chance of selling your pitch.

> Don't forget the passion!

One thing I often notice is missing in some guests: passion. Enthusiasm. A joy in what you are doing. Passion sells, but passion doesn't need to smother. I don't need to be over-sold that you are passionate. If you are passionate—it will simply sell. I'll think twice about booking a passionless guest even if they have a killer hook! Remember, television is show business, and when we get right down to it, this is all about performance. Dull presentation tarnishes the gleam of even a fascinating subject. But you know what? You are reading *Get on TV,* so you are on the right path to recognize and achieve your goals.

Chapter 4

Building a Solid Platform

Miracles Can Happen: Paul's Story

"Good Morning. Theta Cable."

"Yes, this is Paul Ryan and I'd like to host a TV talk show."

"Yes, Mr. Ryan. When would you like to start?"

"I'll be down in a half hour."

For Paul Ryan, it really was as easy as picking up a phone and asking for a TV show. And twenty-five years later, he has done on-air interviews with hundreds of celebrities, such as Robin Williams, Jerry Seinfeld, Jay Leno, Sophia Loren, Jack Lemmon, Johnny Carson, Brooke Shields, Robert Blake, Kylie Minogue, and Hilary Swank. He went on to become the series host of L.A.'s morning TV talk show, Hollywood correspondent for *Entertainment Tonight*, series host of the game show *Love Thy Neighbor*, emcee of charity fundraisers, and host/producer of a new series, *Feel-Good TV with Paul Ryan and Friends.*

How's that for career exposure? And Paul Ryan literally got his start as a celebrity interviewer by picking up the phone and asking for the job. "They said, 'Fine. When do you want to start?'" he recalls, "I was totally blown away. I expected some resistance." There is no exaggeration in this story, but there is some omission as to the nature of Theta Cable.

Can you guess Theta Cable's "secret?" No peeking. Got your answer? Stumped? Check back later in this very chapter and all will be revealed...

Good News, Bad News

We've come to a place in our relationship where I feel I can level with you all.

Brace yourselves.

Ready? OK, truth time. By now, you have hopefully accepted that getting on TV is a very real possibility for many of you with something unique or interesting to offer. You believe booking will happen and you are planning to implement the tips in this book and get out there into the middle of the fray and pitch your heart out. That's the good news: yes, you can do it. And now for the bad, or maybe merely not as good news.

Just because you are ready doesn't mean the world is ready and waiting to hear your pitch. There almost certainly will be obstacles ahead.

What's that you say? How dare I go four chapters and tell you this now? *Because this process takes a lot of hard work, persistence, and quiet patience.* Can it happen overnight? Yes. I book first-timers every single week, many first-timers. But that's my end of the equation. To all of you reading this book: some of you will get lucky, some of you will not. *Get on TV* is intended to help you maximize your chances of getting booked. Booking lightning cannot strike you if you are hiding in the basement, dreaming of taking your act on TV.

So think of the book as a portable lightning rod or a lucky rabbit's foot. It will absolutely bring luck and opportunity your way. But, of course, you have to have your act together. I can point you in all the right directions and give you last-minute marching orders, but only you can follow through. In this chapter, we'll get into more detail about following through with your goal to be on TV by *building your platform.*

PLATFORM

Your platform is the action behind your business plan that backs what you do and what you claim you can do.

Counting Chickens: The Psychic's Story

Recently, my office was contacted by a young woman who pitched herself as a psychic medium. Actually, she doesn't like the word "medium," and might I note that she did not have an alternate name of choice, but, yes, she talks to the dead. I think it takes a tremendous amount of bravery to try and carve out a career in this profession in the first place, but to then admit that you want to do this *publicly* takes even more courage and fortitude.

After years of pondering her options, our psychic friend decided "I want this now," and so she expects things to happen *right now.* But although you may decide to switch careers and become an ER nurse, you still have to do the training. Every career path has prerequisites, a checklist of basic experiences that one needs under their belt before claiming proficiency.

The recent popularity of John Edward's *Crossing Over* and James Van Praagh's show *Beyond* (both now cancelled) has given encouragement to a lot of other psychic mediums. Some want their own show, some want to be professional TV guestperts, others wish to pen a series of books on their subject.

The problem *is* that everyone who has ever dreamt of a dead relative now claims to be a psychic medium. So the challenge for our psychic friend, a mother of four from Indiana, is simple, yet challenging: she has to separate herself from the pack. She has to have a unique angle. More important, she has to create a carefully crafted platform based on a body of media experience and appearances. If you're psychic and you want me to book you, you *have to have an angle,* and you have to have a platform. You could call me up and tell me what socks I am wearing, what I want to eat for lunch, and what I was just thinking about when the phone rang, but unless you have a hook for my show and have demonstrated some credibility publicly, whether through speaking, writing, radio, or television, there's little I can do other than stand in awe of your ability.

Building your platform, shaping the media profile you are seeking is going to take a lot of trial and error and time. It is imperative that you remember this:

> You need to show us what you've *got,* not just what you *do.*

So it was back to the drawing board for our psychic friend. The lesson here is don't count your chickens before they hatch. Building a platform is crucial. Planning and preparation (that word again!) are absolutely essential to success.

> ## THERE IS NO SHAME IN CANCELLATION
>
> It is important to realize that cancellation does not always equate with "failure." In the case of *Crossing Over* and *Beyond*, the pop culture cycle for "speaking with the departed" merely ran its natural course in syndication. For example, *Who Wants to be a Millionaire* became massively popular almost overnight, stayed high in the ratings game for months, then came to the end of its pop cultural "hot" cycle within a year. Just because it got cancelled does not mean that game shows are "out." So if your specialty is spiritual contact, now is the time to think up a fresh hook for a *Crossing Over* successor show.

Building Credibility

Coming up with your platform and resulting hooks is much the same as coming up with a business plan. Your investors (we, the producers of

America) want to know if you are what you say you are and that you can put your money where your mouth is. If you are pitching to me, you are essentially asking *me* to put *my money* where *your mouth is*. Maybe you have a great pitch and an array of catchy seasonal and topical hooks planned out. Great, but what are you doing to back them up?

If you are a Washington insider, can you deliver any good dirt, scandal, or gossip? If you are a vegan chef, do non-vegans really love your food? If you are a nutritionist with a new diet plan, can you show us anybody who has used it to lose a significant, no, make that a dramatic, amount of weight? If you are a defense lawyer who takes on hopeless cases, can you share a story that's entertaining and dramatic, one that makes a good tale in the telling?

PLATFORM

To repeat: Your platform is the action behind your business plan that backs what you do and what you claim you can do.

I'll book a Joe Regular with a solid platform rather than a flashy, more telegenic person with the same pitch and no experience. Since producers have all the responsibility of how a show turns out, we want to make safe bets. If you have no show reel, no press kit, and no media experience or exposure, chances are I'll move on to the next potential guest rather than book you. Or I'll just have my researcher, booker, or associate producers find me somebody with your pitch who has a firm platform.

How to Market Yourself: The Five-Finger Brand Hand

Other than her unusual ability, our psychic friend had confidence going for her, but little else that was practical. As a media consultant I believed her self-declared experience, but producers? They would need more. Much more. What she needed to establish was a solid, well-developed platform. In turn, her platform would create a presence for her that would speak for itself.

I have a straightforward marketing strategy for you, courtesy of entertainment business manager and producer Angelica Holiday. She calls it the "Five-Finger Brand Hand." I think it is an excellent strategy that you can use to build your platform.

The Five-Finger Brand Hand should answer the question, "What is my presence in..."

1. The Internet?
2. Speaking?
3. Print?
4. Radio?
5. Television?

Begin to build your repertoire as an expert in all these areas. Offer your services and practice what you preach.

1. The Internet

Talk show host, model, and actress Cindy Margolis rose to national attention for being the "most downloaded woman" on the Internet when having your own web page was becoming popular. Cindy took her modeling career in her own hands, by making her web page her store front. She has gone on to host her own talk show, star in movies, and has made a full brand out of her blonde bombshell appearance.

Most television producers use the Internet as their main research tool. It is considered as commonplace an expectation to have a web page of your own as it would be to have a business card. It's an easy place for producers to look up your bio and photo. Not that there is truth to the perception of this, but truly, a web page gives a potential TV guestpert instant credibility.

TVGUESTPERT.COM

If you don't have a web page of your own, a TV guestpert can list his or her profile on this fee-based site, which is marketed to television producers. The service is run by Jacquie Jordan Inc.

2. Speaking

As far as speaking engagements go, church groups and other organizations are great places to start out, but don't expect to be paid.

Case Study: The Doula

First, let's define terms. A *doula* is a professional midwife and birth expert. They teach expectant mothers breathing techniques, prepare them mentally and physically for the birth experience, and help them through the birth itself. Doulas mediate between old-school/old-world (and therefore timeless) ideas about birth and birthing and medical science's approach, which is often accused of being a little too clinical and remote. They help make hospital births more mother-friendly, and also assist with deliveries at birthing centers and even home births.

Giuditta Tornetta is a Los Angeles–based birth doula, and the soon-to-be published author of *Joy in Birthing*. Her pitch is: *It's a mother's right to have a natural and painless childbirth.* Her hook is: *Not only did she do it for herself when she gave birth to her own daughter at home, but she has coached several clients to do the same.* In building her platform, Giuditta began by giving free lectures at hospitals, through the Whole Foods grocery store chain, and in the living rooms of mothers and their friends. She tested her radio and television material out in small venues, and signed up with a speaker's bureau. As she crafted her information presentation and began to build her business, she signed up to write a monthly column in the *Los Angeles Family Magazine*, and has kept fresh columns up on her website.

SPEAKERS BUREAU

A company that represents speakers of every description and takes client bookings for conferences, meetings, seminars, and other events.

GET ON TV TIP:

Speakers bureaus are an amazing resource that I highly recommend. There are scores of them, so go online and get Googling!

As Giuditta created and expanded her presence in the local community through public speaking, her business and client base began to grow concurrently with her platform. She created a nonprofit venture for mothers who couldn't afford doula services, all to back the pitch on which the foundation of her business was built—*It's a mother's right to have a natural and painless childbirth.*

Of the points in the Five-Finger Brand Hand, Giuditta began with speaking, segued into Internet, then print, then radio, and TV requests subsequently followed! All of this was initially a local phenomenon. To reference popular culture (*Field of Dreams*) in relation to your platform— "If you build it, they will come."

3. Print

The print option has multiple avenues of approach, from free local community newspapers to having your own pamphlets printed out for sale or to give away. All such experience is useful. Think of this as the "spread your wings" phase before actual flight into more high-impact, large-market media.

And as producers, we all take pride in discovering that bargain at a flea market, or an obscure author, book, musical artist, or movie that we just have to spread the word about. It's no different in the booking game. I believe I've found a diamond in the rough when I find information about someone intriguing in a small newspaper, or in a magazine item, or on a local news show. There is something fresh, attractive, and exciting in discovering "new talent." The big expectations about your TV appearances are great to have, but often I've seen it inhibit guests from enjoying the process. Sometimes, the journey itself is more fun than the actual destination.

I booked Angela Moore of Newport, Rhode Island, on *Donny & Marie* because I saw this tiny article about her fun jewelry in *InStyle* magazine. This was a few years ago. Today, I see her work in many catalogs and magazine fashion spreads.

If you strategize yourself correctly, print media can be a valuable and powerful tool for elevating your profile. Some people are understandably eager to leap straight onto television, and that's fine, but it doesn't always work out for them in the long run. Your career as a TV guest or expert may run its course in a booking or two, then, if you really believe in what you are doing and want to make it a permanent part of your life, you have to head back to square one: internet, print, local radio, etc. By ignoring the initial steps to a solid platform, you may get the short-term thrill of a few major bookings, but the long-term advantage might fail to materialize. Angela Moore is one of the fortunate ones: she was able to capitalize on her early TV appearances, which in turn were based on one tiny print reference in a magazine.

THINK PRINT! CHECKLIST

1. Find out what your available local and regional print options are; the Internet is a good source for this.
2. Apply your hook and pitch yourself to the appropriate editor.
3. Have a press release available at all times. Be sure to have it proofread by someone adept in the intricacies of the English language; editors hate bad syntax!
4. Always have a recent photograph ready. What would be the point to attract media attention and not have them see what you look like?

4. Radio

Here's an idea for radio exposure that you may be able to adapt for your area. L.A.'s Pacifica station is part of a larger network of Public Broadcasting stations. It's very, very left of center, but as a consequence, the programming is wildly divergent, from political analysis by experts to do-it-yourself shows where the "man in the street" chips in his (or her) two cents. There are programs about astrology, cooking, music, and various documentary shows (tracing the history of Blues music, for example). Whatever your pitch may be, from sexologist to numerologist, from chef to fitness consultant, there are potential hooks for any number of preexisting shows. You may have freewheeling stations like Pacifica in your area. Look into the local college's radio programming and see if there are any shows suited to you. You may get "no's" everywhere, but you will benefit from exercising that mental creativity muscle. Even if it's a lost cause, coming up with multiple hooks for a variety of shows will serve you well when you get to the television stage, or even to the next tier up in radio, the AM talk radio formats.

5. Television

There's even a back-door way for getting onto TV. Remember celebrity interviewer and multimedia jack-of-all-trades Paul Ryan?

Paul's Story Continued and the Mystery of the Instant TV Hosting Job

It's time to resolve our mystery cliffhanger. How did Paul land his own celebrity interview television show simply by picking up the phone and asking for the job? Does he possess hypnotic powers of suggestion? Was Theta Cable playing a prank, one that ironically backfired when Paul actually became a celebrity interviewer? Were they that hard up that they'd hire him *sight unseen?*

The answer to all these questions is a resounding "no."

What Paul Ryan didn't know when he picked up the phone to call Theta Cable, is that it was a *public access station*. Starting in 1972, the Federal Communications Commission (FCC) required all cable systems to provide one channel for public access usage. The companies were also required to furnish free facilities and basic equipment for public use. *This means that anyone who wants a show (wants to be on TV) has legal access to this space.*

Paul was given one hour a week of commercial-free airtime, two volunteer cameramen, and, he jokes, "A set the size of a broom closet, two chairs you could find at a garage sale, and a couple of rubber plants that have seen better days." He then had to produce his own show *from scratch*. He had to figure out how to book celebrity guests (hint: start small and work your way up), and how to introduce, present, and pace his hour-length show. The first weeks had the ramshackle feel of an impromptu kids' talent show in a family basement, but from this most humble of beginnings on public access cable TV, *which is available to all of us,* he was eventually picked up by the Satellite Program Network, where he could be seen in 650 cities, and in three million homes.

Needless to say, local public access cable is a great way to get started. You can practice your act and nobody will hold your initial stumbles against you. Fair warning: Different states and cities have different standards of acceptable behavior. Some public access shows may feature material that may offend some people. So, while researching your local PA channels' shows, just be prepared to change channels! This sort of programming, which is arguably made possible under First Amendment rights to free speech, represents a minority of PA programming. Just be warned in case grandma or the kids are helping you build your platform by doing some TV research!

Your Dress Rehearsal: Local Media Markets

Living in Los Angeles, I tell clients to try out smaller markets in Sacramento, Las Vegas, Phoenix, or Santa Barbara. These are places that are local and relatively nearby. They aren't as high a risk as the #2 market of L.A. Get yourself out there. Test your material. Test your pitches. *You don't want to put your best foot forward and find out you aren't even ready.* You can't blow a pitch to a producer and then beg for a second chance. If they didn't trust your pitch in the first place, why would they trust you to deliver on air? There is no way to make a second first impression, unless you go away and radically rework what it is that you are doing. I keep repeating this advice in different contexts because I see so many well meaning and enthusiastic people fail due to inexperience or ill-preparation. I want you to put your best foot forward.

There's a famous slogan that relates to being politically active:

"Think global, act local."

So if you are concerned about pollution and the global environment, for example, your work should begin in your own backyard. The "think global, act local" motto is useful in almost any context, and as we have already touched upon several times, it's also vitally relevant to building your platform of experience.

Let's start practicing right now. If you don't know the answers, set yourself the task of finding out ASAP. *Know your terrain, master the map.* Get off on a good foot, kiddos!

STUDY GUIDE

What is your local public access cable channel?
What is your local newspaper?
What is your local magazine?

Remember, many smaller markets (i.e., not major population centers) produce their own local shows. Some may be dicey, but many are extremely well produced and in touch with their audience's needs and interests.

Attack print media with the same strategy and verve that you will eventually apply to national televisions shows. *Television producers derive the majority of their ideas from the print media—magazines and newspapers.* As I stated before, when it's in print, we think we've discovered something fresh. So don't underestimate getting yourself written up...or writing yourself up. For this, I recommend starting locally. A multitude of small publications in your area exist (cast your regional net wide, if need be) and are considered to be fantastic resources for hungry producers. Getting an article in print is also a great way to try out your hook and analyze what you did right and maybe could have improved. Then of course, once it's in print, you can color-copy it and add it to your press kit. Exposure in print only adds to your credibility.

Going National

At the National Association of Television Programming Executives, I had the opportunity to moderate a couple of dynamic panels. During a Q&A session, an audience member expressed his frustration as to why his fishing TV show, which had been on the air for fourteen years, hadn't been picked up "in Hollywood." There are thousands of reasons that this could be, but the point that I think was overlooked was this: he has been producing this show about his passion in life, and it's been on the air for *a decade and a half*! What's to complain about? To a viewer, if you are on TV, you are on TV: it's a big deal.

I didn't speak with this gentleman at great length, but I would imagine given the locality of where he is from, a fishing show works well regionally. I'm sure he might feel that if the show were seen nationally, he would earn more money. That may or may not be true, especially in this business. He could go wide, flop spectacularly, and leave his backers out-of-pocket. His most important ancillary opportunity is his platform, not his channel real estate.

Let's take another real-life example to illustrate our major points here. We'll stick with the "Go fish!" theme.

The pitch: a fishing show. The hook: jazz musician and actor John Lurie goes fishing with his celebrity pals. What's the platform? Lurie is underground and ultra hip. As the show *Fishing with John* was for the Independent Film Channel (IFC), Lurie's "celebrity pals" encompassed a wide array of alternate cinema stars, like musician Tom Waits as well as better-known faces such as Matt Dillon, Willem Dafoe, and Dennis Hopper. Another important angle or hook was that the show was only concerned with fishing in passing. Its hilariously deadpan narration was imitative of those over-earnest programs you see on the social habits of leaf bugs of the Kalahari.

So here we have a fine example of how to design a fishing show that will have national appeal. *Fishing with John* took a creative approach and is now available on DVD over ten years after its initial run on IFC. The lesson here is to honestly appraise your efforts, from pitch to hook to platform. Our fisherman host with the astonishing fourteen-year run on regional television was assuming that what works in Vermont will work as well in San Francisco, Austin, Tampa, and Portland. That may not be so, unless you have something fresh to offer.

Be creative with your hooks. Train yourself to look at other shows or guests or products and imagine other ways that they could have been pitched. What would you do differently? What do you think works? What needs improvement? Make a habit of brainstorming. How would you pitch yourself to the most unlikely television venue? By imagining what's possible and even what's improbable, you will train your mind to *think outside the box* and think like a TV producer would about you.

Thinking outside the box means that you are removing yourself from the constraints of conventional wisdom in an effort to see new possibilities and fresh ideas. The visionaries who developed the pull-down menus (aka *user interfaces*) that every computer uses were thinking outside of the box. So was da Vinci. And Einstein.

Be sure to inventory the total gamut of your plan. It helps to be fully organized with a firm foundation. In every field of human endeavor, it is individuals thinking outside the box who move their chosen area forward. There is no reason why your efforts should be any different.

Also, do your research. Find out what others like you are doing. Be aware that many similar ideas crop up in the zeitgeist of creative evolution, so you don't want to put a lot of time into something without knowing what the competition is doing too.

No matter whether you are a chef or a lawyer or a tax accountant, taking a revolutionary approach to your pitch, hooks, and platform building is something that anybody can train themselves to do.

Stand out from the crowd.

Be novel.

Be unique.

Create an underground revolution and attract television producers to you!

CHECKLIST: INVENTORY YOUR PLAN

Let's take an inventory, because without a solid foundation, your platform will be weak.
- What is your platform?
- How are you executing your platform?
- Do you have your five-finger branding plan in place, in order to execute your platform?

And remember to:
- Think small.
- Think print.
- Think local.

Building a solid, credible platform by targeting your local community through a variety of media (the Internet, speaking, print, radio, and television) helps with the strategic process to get on TV. Aspiring TV guest-perts have the opportunity to work out the kinks of their business, attract new clients, work out hooks and pitches, and morph into a solid brand name that can't help but make TV come crawling to them.

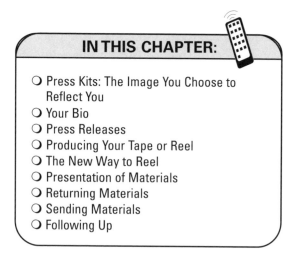

Chapter 5

Press Kits and Show Reels: The Importance of Tape and Materials

IN THIS CHAPTER:

- ○ Press Kits: The Image You Choose to Reflect You
- ○ Your Bio
- ○ Press Releases
- ○ Producing Your Tape or Reel
- ○ The New Way to Reel
- ○ Presentation of Materials
- ○ Returning Materials
- ○ Sending Materials
- ○ Following Up

A few years ago, I was all set to teach one of my media seminars. The company that was sponsoring the event forwarded a package to me from a registered seminar participant. I didn't bother opening the package, not because I was busy, but because the item, quite frankly, freaked me out.

The package was wrapped in a dirty brown paper bag, secured with string and ratty duct tape. Newspaper stuffing was bursting out from the corners. My name was hastily scribbled on the package's front, and I doubt that even the FBI's best handwriting experts could make sense of the return address.

Why didn't I open the package? Are you kidding me? It might as well have had Unabombers-R-Us written on it! Well, OK, I'm exaggerating; I did not believe that the package was dangerous. But had it been sent to one of the shows that I work on, it would have been dumped for just such a reason. In our post-9/11 world, suspicious packages are not taken lightly.

I reluctantly brought the fleabag package with me to the seminar, in hopes that I might review the contents with the sender, who had, after all, paid his entry fee for the event.

After the seminar class concluded, the gentleman who sent the package introduced himself. He was upset with me for not looking at his materials ahead of time. He took the trouble to send it in early, and he had been hoping for direct feedback during the seminar that would aid him and his cause.

He was right. I could have helped him immensely had I reviewed his material. But the fact remains that I still will not open a package wrapped like that. And to tell the truth, had I received the package at the studio, I would have just thrown it away.

The gentleman got what he wanted in the end: after all, I do what I do to help people get their stories out. And lucky for both of us, I did not throw the unappealing package away. The gentleman turned out to be a Holocaust survivor, and inside were *original copies of personal pictures* and poetry that he had written about his experiences. I was amazed and awed by his bravery and his almost unbelievable experiences. I was also privately aghast—what if I had dumped the suspicious package containing these treasures in the nearest trash can based on its outer appearances?

What I've come to believe is that the materials of a pitch are important, if not essential, to the sell because television is a visual medium. The spoken word is the key medium of communication, but in order to get to the point where you are on TV, you have to get in the front door and past the maitre d'. In other words, we producers may refuse your service if your materials are poorly presented. Consider them a reflection of your perceived on-camera delivery.

Put yourself in my place. If you were hiring interns, would you pick the well-spoken, neatly dressed candidate, or the charming yet slovenly one who shows up with uncombed hair and food stains on her shirt, smelling like an ashtray? Your pitch presentation materials are no different!

As I said before in regards to getting booked, *presentation* is nine-tenths of the law. Spiffy makes a good impression, scruffy is a turnoff. Make your pitch materials count. Make them reflect the essence of who and what you are trying to convey. And as we are about to see, this is not an expensive process at all. Far from it.

Press Kits: The Image You Choose to Reflect You

You simply must have a press kit, dah-lings, they're all the rage!

Seriously, there is simply no getting around this part of your assignment. Your press kit, also known as a media kit, is your calling card. It's a means of directly introducing yourself via mail and making that crucial first impression a favorable one. Remember, your initial forays into the world of television bookings will almost certainly not involve cold-calling producers with any degree of success. The press kit is the calling card. Without this essential piece, consider yourself a dead giveaway as being an outsider. If we like the press kit, *then* we pick up the phone.

All press kits contain the same basic components:
- A brief biography (aka "bio")
- A press release stating your pitch, hook, platform, and mission statement
- Press clippings from your prior media experiences (if any)
- A headshot (no Polaroids, please!) of your lovely self
- A business card
- A VHS show reel

Even if you have not yet appeared on television, you can make your own audition tape—an interview with yourself, so to speak (more on this later). All of these materials need to fit neatly into a single folder. What kind of folder? The most basic kind on offer at Staples or Office Depot.

Case Study: The Dumpster Diva

An effective press kit should take what you do, your platform and mission statement, and reflect that essence in the details of the packet.

One of my favorite press kits of all time comes from the "Dumpster Diva." The minute I saw her press kit, I knew *exactly* what she was about. I could gage her level of creativity and passion for her platform, pitch, and hook. Her hook is: *Where most people see garbage, she sees art.*

The Dumpster Diva's press kit instantly demonstrates that she is both a natural communicator and a gifted artist. The kit's cover is very rudimentary, like an art project of a child. It is embellished with construction paper cutout shapes and beads that form her "Dumpster Diva" logo. Now don't get jealous! Some people have a natural knack for art: most do not. I can just about handle a smiley face, but beyond that, all bets are off!

Inside the press kit are color photocopies of the Dumpster Diva's artwork extraordinaire. She transforms cigar boxes into kitsch purses. Her father's old ties become an eye-catching skirt. Boat propellers are retasked as object d'art lamps, and even beer bottle caps find a groovy second life as art deco fridge magnets.

Her press kit is playful, scrappy, and made out of materials she uses in her Dumpster Diva art projects. All materials in the kit are labeled with a Diva logo sticker with her name, address, and phone number.

WHERE DO I GET LOGO STICKERS AND OTHER CUSTOM PRINTED MATERIALS?

Thanks to the explosion of computing power and software in recent years, the cost of custom designing and printing everything from books to posters to logos is now affordable.

Kinko's offers such services, as will many copy stores. Software products also allow you to create logos on your home computer.

Let's recap. Diva's pitch is to bring bohemian beatnik craft and living ideas to the Gen X audience, her hook (for the original appearance) is that she used a thousand bottle caps off the street to make an American flag for the Fourth of July, and her mission statement is that there is no such thing as garbage; anything used can be re-used for art! Her platform is that she was teaching her craft to women in domestic violence shelters. As a result of her initial success, Sonya, the Dumpster Diva, has rebranded herself as SonyaStyle.com and is taking a more mature approach to her brand.

Case Study: Stops Crying Guaranteed

Years ago, I received a press kit in the mail. A disclaimer on the kit read: "You are about to let loose the most annoying yet innocent sound known to the human race. Just raise this lid and hear it, open here."

I opened the box containing the kit and *it screamed and cried like a baby*! This press kit had my immediate and undivided attention...

The sender was Terry Woodford, a former hit record producer and songwriter. He created and developed music therapy tapes to help crying babies fall asleep. His package was filled with products that read, "Stops crying guaranteed." His bio, business card, product information, and other materials about the creator were clearly marked, but all in all this package got my attention. I understood clearly the pitch "Stops crying guaranteed."

This hook and his press kit were so unique and dramatic that I've carried it around from office to office for years. I never did personally find the opportunity to book Terry on TV, but I did pass his materials around to every producer I know and that circulation paid off for Terry.

Today his products are everywhere, and I've seen them featured in magazines and on the news. I should point out that Terry's ultimate goal was to get media attention to sell the CDs. He could have been booked to sell his products, or as a cranky baby expert, or even as somebody who had turned from one career (songwriting and producing) to another (baby care). The point is this: even if you just want to sell Product X or Service Y, keep an eye open for avenues that connect what you are selling to a wider array of topics and pitches.

The following are examples of press kits that I believe capture the essence of the TV guestpert that they represent. Decide for yourself. Even though the area of expertise overlaps, the uniqueness of each individual and his or her style comes through with credibility. And again, the press kit needs to translate into what this TV guestpert would bring to television.

Former model turned lifestyle expert and creator of The A-List.com, Allison Dickson's press kit reflects her fun-loving, free-spirit, "I want to know her beauty secrets" style...

Jonathon Fong of JonathonFongStyle.com created a press kit by using fabric to reflect his style...

Shalini Vadhera of ShaliniVadhera.com, makeup stylist, uses a simpler approach. Even though she has a plain cover—the inside of her press kit highlights her talents and credits.

Cheryl Sindell of CherylSindell.com, nutritionist, uses an entirely custom-designed press kit. Her photo, bio, and name are graphically inclusive.

"But Jacquie," you may now be thinking, "how do I know if my press kit is good enough?" What you need to do is ask yourself two key questions and think carefully and honestly about your answers. Common sense will see you through the process.

The two questions are:

1. Does my press kit project the essence of what I want to impress upon a show producer?

The purpose of the press kit is to establish your image and translate your credibility.

Some of you may wish to spend more money on your press kit folder. The fancier ones that I have received are custom made to include specially designed logos. Those of you on a budget, worry not! Even a leather-bound press kit with a gold embossed logo will fail to register if the materials inside are not up to par. If you haven't followed the *Get on TV* steps for getting booked (i.e., building a platform, starting local), then no matter how fancy the press kit cover is, the materials inside won't reflect the credibility of your creation. In other words, a fancy folder won't fool anybody.

2. What type of information do the producers I am targeting need from me in order to do their job?

A long and detailed bio regaling us with colorful tales from high school or your place of employment might give me an indication of your personality, but if this information does not specifically tie into your pitch, then it is irrelevant. Your press kit is not an essay or a short story. It should be direct and to the point and should contain your pitch, hook, and platform via the materials included.

Your Bio

A bio is the first thing to include in your press kit materials. CVs or resumes, traditional biographies, and author biographies are going to miss the point. We want to know who you are before we invite you over to our "house." Nothing fancy, just the facts.

- Your basic credentials as they relate to your pitch.
- A brief history of your involvement in your area of expertise.
- A colorful detail illustrating your suitability to your specialty.
- Most important, what is your essence?

To capture the essence in a biography is very important, but difficult as it relates to yourself. When I work with clients, I try to find an interesting and unique personal hook that would be interesting to a hopeful TV producer.

One client, "Don the Music Man," who is remarkably talented and plays music to inner-city schoolchildren, couldn't find a personal angle that made him interesting. When interviewing Don, I discovered that he was the youngest of eighteen children from a gospel-singing family in Mississippi. The youngest of eighteen children. I don't know anyone like that nowadays. I lead with that in his bio.

Born in Jackson, Mississippi, as the youngest of 18 children, Don Herron was motivated at a very young age to capture the attention of his musically talented family. Shortly after his mother began to give him voice and piano lessons, she recognized that her youngest son was gifted. His ability to play piano by ear even before learning to read music, coupled with his outstanding voice, prepared him to make his early start playing gospel music at local churches. Don continued to hone his skills throughout grade school, singing classical, jazz, rhythm and blues, and show tunes with various bands and groups on local television shows.

High school opened the door to many other artistic opportunities for Don, including playing trombone in the marching band and performing in such plays as *Oklahoma, The Music Man*, and *Lil' Abner*, just to name a few. Don also had a talent for sports, and soon became known for his State Championship title in tennis, which took his career in a different direction. He boarded a Greyhound bus by the age of 19, and headed for Los Angeles to play for the L.A. Trade-Tech College, where he was soon to score another Championship title.

Although his days at L.A. Trade-Tech were spent on the tennis court, he continued to pursue his love of music at the Long Beach City College, where he was accompanied by such artists as Patrice Rushen, Kenny Burrell, the late Dizzy Gillespie, and Wilton Felder. He became well known in the gospel community and spent his weekends performing at the House of Blues in Hollywood. Don has traveled throughout the U.S. and Alaska, touring as Music Director in many theatrical productions featuring artists Yolanda Adams, Vicky Winans, Shirley Caesar, and more.

Don shares his talents now with the next generation of budding musicians. His ability to imitate the sounds of several instruments with theatrical presence has earned him the name "The Music Man" with his younger crowd. His lessons in children's music and movement can be enjoyed at many preschools throughout Southern California.

Your bio should ideally fit onto one page, but another half page is fair enough. If you make it longer, you are pushing the limits of most producers' attentions. I usually do not read beyond the first paragraph, so don't ramble. Get to the point right away.

In Michelle Flores's case, she is a dynamic television personality; however, she's an employment litigator. Kind of dry given her presence. How can we make this woman jump off the page beyond her expertise? I wanted to know why she had a passion for this work.

Here is her professional biography—impressive, but dry for television.

Michelle Lee Flores

Michelle Lee Flores focuses her practice on employment matters, including litigation and compliance, and labor and business litigation. She serves as primary counsel in all aspects of litigation, including jury and bench trials, arbitration and mediation involving wrongful termination, employment discrimination, Internet and multimedia issues, copyright, trademark, unfair competition claims, and various general business and entertainment disputes.

Areas of Experience
Labor and employment law
Intellectual property litigation
General business litigation
Commercial litigation
Significant representations

- Advise and counsel directors of human resources on various employment matters, including internal investigation, discipline, termination, FMLA, CFRA, PDL and other leave requirements, and wage and hour matters in all industries.
- Prepare position statements for the California Department of Fair Employment and Housing, and California Department of Labor Standards Enforcement, and represent employers in administrative hearings.
- Advise executives concerning employment issues, including negotiation of separation agreements.
- Draft employment contracts, employee handbooks, personnel policy manuals, drug testing policies, separation agreements, arbitration agreements, applications for employment, and a variety of employer notices.
- Prepare advisory opinions on complex labor and employment issues.
- Interpret and provide opinions regarding collective bargaining agreements.

Articles

Co-author, "What Every Management Lawyer Should Know about a Plaintiff's Bankruptcy," *California Labor and Employment Law Quarterly*, Winter 1997.

Education

JD, University of California at Los Angeles, 1993
Business Editor, *Federal Communications Law Journal*
Member, Moot Court
BA, *magna cum laude,*Arizona State University, 1990
Member, Phi Beta Kappa; Psi Chi; Alpha Lambda Delta
Member, Golden Key National Honor Society
Arizona Regents Scholarship Recipient

The purpose of the television biography is to put into words the essence of what we would expect this TV guestpert to be on camera. The above biography, although thorough, would be quite a dry personality if it translated directly to TV, albeit a smart one.

Michelle Lee Flores
(Not Your Typical) Litigator

She's a spitfire on TV just as she is in the courtroom! With 10-plus years of litigation experience, attorney Michelle Lee Flores champions causes for employers and employees with a sense of righteousness and justice. You not only want her on your side, but you pity her opposing counsel.

When only 11 years old, Michelle was present in court when her mother defended herself in an employment lawsuit. Unable to testify on her mother's behalf, and recognizing that neither she nor her mother knew the proper legal procedures, Michelle experienced a significant sense of helplessness at a tender age. Her experience in the courtroom has led her to her passion as a crusader of employment related rights for both employers and employees.

Michelle's experience is in civil litigation and her expertise is in employment law. She also has a significant practice advising employers on employment compliance matters. As a seasoned courtroom veteran, Michelle can speak on a variety of topics in the news, such as wrongful termination, employment discrimination, sexual harassment, unfair competition claims, business disputes, procedural matters in all civil litigation matters, Internet and multimedia issues, and various general business and entertainment disputes. Michelle has argued hundreds of

matters in court and has successfully tried jury trials, bench trials, and binding arbitrations, as well as successfully resolving
numerous lawsuits through mediation. Most recently, she was
named one of Southern California's "Rising Star Super
Lawyers" for 2004 and was nominated as one of Southern
California's "Super Lawyers" for 2004.

"I like to think of myself as a helper to my client—a problem solver. Once a dispute has reached the point of a lawsuit,
most people think of lawyers as problem makers."

Michelle has a unique way of looking at her job, particularly in her representation of employers. "I believe that most
employers want to comply with the employment rules that are
out there, but many are just uninformed or misguided. In general, I think that 50 percent of the claims made against
employers are legitimate, and 50 percent are not. What concerns me is that of the legitimate claims made, there are even
more out there that employees do not raise with their employers. In addition, I am incensed by unfounded claims as they
reduce the credibility of legitimate ones."

Michelle currently practices employment law and civil litigation at Greenberg Traurig, LLP.

Michelle's philosophy is to maintain integrity and credibility while vigorously advocating for her clients. She also recog-
nizes that reputations, careers, and livelihoods are on the line
with the work that she does.

In assisting clients on creating their television biography, I interview
them about their field of expertise. I am also interested in knowing who
they are and what makes them tick. We often draw upon our personal
experiences to become the professionals that we are. The bios should separate them from the pack of other professionals whose credits are similar.
As a producer, I am looking for those TV guestperts whose uniqueness

would make them interesting to my television audience. The challenging part of constructing our own bio is that we take for granted or don't often see our own unique personal hook. When writing my own bio, I always seek an outside perspective that can lend fresh eyes to content that I might otherwise take for granted.

Press Releases

Extra! Extra! Read all about it…. A press release is the next major print element in your press kit. Think of this as the "birth announcement" heralding your arrival on the television scene. It should tell a producer what's new, what's exciting, and what's happening with you and your field. Dry recitation is out. Make the press release as vivacious as possible without veering into loud hyperbole. Enthusiasm is the key word here.

What a Press Release Looks Like

A press release is the urgent message that you want to convey in your media kit. It should have a timely ring to it and share details of the who, where, and what is happening in your world. It's essentially your news story insert packaged inside your press kit. The press release should contain all the basic facts with a titillating headline, followed by a strong lead-in paragraph. To a producer, a press release is the two-page pitch of what I would be putting you on TV for and what the viewer would get out of it.

- Press releases should be newsworthy, not an advertisement.
- Give producers concise information.
- Let producers know why their audience needs this information.
- Your headline and your lead-in paragraph are most important.
- Stick to the facts, not the fluff.
- Include a release date or mark the press release "For immediate release."
- Number the pages.
- Write "End" or denote the end when finished (for example, ###).
- And most important, make sure your contact information is included on every page.

See how a press release helped get an important message out for this TV guestpert's client.

Case Study: Manuel Velasco

Once upon a time (but not all that long ago), Manuel Velasco arrived at Los Angeles Airport (LAX) ready to board a flight to Washington State, where he was planning to visit his younger brother.

Manuel was transporting a box of his brother's possessions along with his own luggage. Imagine Manuel's shock when he suddenly found himself surrounded and detained by armed LAX airport security guards! A CTX scan of the box revealed that it contained a *hand grenade*…a replica in fact, as it was soon determined. Manuel's younger brother collected military memorabilia and had completely forgotten that the replica was in that particular box. In fact, he had forgotten he even owned such a thing.

Now, Manuel did not mind being detained or missing his flight: not in the least. He felt awful that he had inadvertently created such havoc. But there were *thousands* of people at LAX airport at that hour and every last one of them were herded outside the terminals due to the security alert triggered by the initial report of a grenade in a passenger's luggage. Scores of travelers missed flights as they stood outside for hours.

For inconveniencing so many people, Manuel Velasco felt deeply embarrassed and ashamed. But then his embarrassment and shame rocketed into the stratosphere when the local and national media picked up the story. Jeering headlines took Manuel to task for such a "stupid" stunt in the post-9/11 era. The thing was, it was not a stunt or a prank, but an honest mistake.

Manuel's detainment brought with it police charges, so he hired criminal defense attorney Anthony V. Salerno to represent him (we'll meet Anthony, who now has a successful media career as a TV legal guestpert in addition to his law practice, later in chapter 9). Anthony's firm, in turn, retained my media consultancy firm to help restore his client's good name and reputation. I had to come up with a hook that would spin the story away from the derisive and abrasive headlines that were assailing Manuel's character, and also allow his attorney, Anthony V. Salerno, to become the official face of the story.

The media's response was understandable: at the time, the whole nation was still skittish about airport security. But a serious issue was being overlooked here in favor of demonizing Manuel. Four experts in airport security reviewed the incident and determined that the CTX scanner operator who initiated the panicked airport shutdown should have been trained to recognize the fake for what it was. In other words, the LAX shutdown was wholly unnecessary. This was taking place against a backdrop of almost weekly stories about poorly trained, overworked and underpaid airport security personnel who were routinely missing guns and knives smuggled onto airplanes by undercover journalists. They can hardly be blamed for such mistakes, but that does not mean that such errors should not be carefully considered.

So we crafted a press release that reflected both the overlooked security issues at stake and Manuel's contrite attitude. He wanted to publicly apologize to his fellow travelers for inconveniencing them and for being so careless. We released his apology in the format of an official statement.

FOR IMMEDIATE RELEASE   CONTACT: JACQUIE JORDAN
                                     310-979-0330

AIRPORT COURT

COLLECTIBLE REPLICA GRENADE CASE

CHALLENGES LAX SECURITY
OFFENDER OFFERS APOLOGY

"He is SINCERELY SORRY for how so many passengers were inconvenienced, but he absolutely had no knowledge that the collectible replica grenade was inside the box, " states criminal defense attorney Anthony V. Salerno, representing suspect Manuel Velasco.

<u>Manuel Velasco will be ARRAIGNED THIS MORNING, MONDAY, MARCH 25TH AT A LOS ANGELES AIRPORT COURT ON LA CIENEGA BLVD., DIVISION 147 AT 8:30AM.</u>

The defense charges that Mr. Velasco is BEING UNFAIRLY SCAPEGOATED FOR THE INEFFICIENCY AND INCOMPETENCY OF LAX SECURITY. According to the Daily Breeze, "four separate experts believe that the operator of the CTX scanning machine was improperly trained, and that a competent CTX operator would have quickly determined that the collectible replica grenade posed no threat."

"Mr. Velasco is NOT GUILTY OF ANY CRIMINAL OFFENSES because he did not know that the box he checked-in contained the collectible replica grenade and that the box belonged to his younger brother which contained his personal effects. Mr. Velasco was taking the box to Washington State to help his younger brother with a planned move. Mr. Velasco's brother was NOT ATTEMPTING TO PLAY A JOKE, he just wasn't thinking."

"Moreover, Secretary of Transportation Norman Mineta called LAX security an 'embarrassment' for its constant shutdowns, including a recent incident where a metal detector machine wasn't even plugged in. Secretary Mineta also said that the response of shutting down two whole terminals was not necessary, and that there needs to be less drastic responses to minor security breaches such as the one involving Mr. Velasco," quotes the defense.

The U.S. Attorney's Office declined to file charges against Mr. Velasco, according to spokesperson Thom Mrozek, in part because they recognized that Mr. Velasco did not know that the collectible replica grenade was inside the box.

"MY CLIENT WANTS TO APOLOGIZE TO HIS FELLOW TRAVELERS WHO WERE PUT OUT AT CURBSIDE FOR SEVERAL HOURS WITHOUT ANY INFORMATION AS TO WHAT WAS GOING ON," states Manuel Velasco's attorney.

###

By playing the "apology" angle of this story—and guess what, people, this angle is a great example of a hook—the law firm was able to get Manuel's apology on TV, where it was watched by millions and had a powerful effect on all those who had been inconvenienced by the incident. As a result, all charges against Manuel were dropped, and he felt that it was understood that his was an honest mistake. Defense attorney Anthony V. Salerno used the media available to all of us to support his client's case.

Press Release Cheat

If you are just starting out on your media career and are not feeling confident enough to write a convincing and official press release, a good back-up strategy is to pose ten imaginary questions relevant to your idea, story, etc., that a TV host might ask you. Make your answers compelling and varied. If you come up short for questions, just turn on the TV and watch the show you are targeting. And don't be too exhaustive or precise: we want an idea of what you might say, but we still want to feel as if we're running the show!

The following is an example of what a press release cheat might look like from a stay-at-home mom/business owner/TV guestpert trying to convey her story to a producer:

CONTACT INFORMATION HERE:

Why don't people get ahead financially when both parents work? Because their expenses quadruple. You are looking at business clothes for both parents, full-time child care, both incomes taxed. It takes a lot more money to support two careers, a household, and the lives of children.

How do mothers handle the transition from the working world to being a full-time mother? It's an adjustment that requires emotional support and creative stimulation.

Why do you think it's more satisfying to be a stay-at-home mother than a working mother? The myth is that a woman who stays at home can't have it all. With technology, there are many ways women can have it all right from her home and neither she, her marriage, nor her children suffer.

What made you decide to work from home? I left a high-profile career where I was making $80,000 a year. The pressure on myself and the family was immense and we were barely breaking even supporting the lifestyle. We sat down with a financial consultant to see how we could make ends meet and found out that it would be more cost-effective if I stayed at home. From there I started a home business and now bring in $120,000 a year with a lot less stress on everybody.

What are the biggest challenges of working from home? For many it's: 1) The discipline of doing it. 2) Not changing environments. 3) Not getting dressed

---

up to go to work. 4) Children can be unpredictable and you often have to work around that.

What are the biggest rewards? Aside from being a mother, which is implicitly rewarding, you are still able to contribute to the workforce, which is satisfying. Plus, you are earning money and contributing to the family income, and most important, you—and not someone else—are raising your children.

How did this transition affect your marriage? It used to be that I was jealous of my husband because he got to go to work, then he became jealous of me because I got to stay home with the kids. Now, we both work at home together.

Do you work at home together on the same business? No. We work in separate industries, but he parlayed what I had learned from working at home into making it work for him.

So how has that affected the family income? We have tripled our income and reduced our debt.

Was having him working from home an adjustment? I'd be lying if I said it wasn't, but we've found a constructive way to share parenting responsibilities and do our jobs.

CONTACT INFORMATION HERE

###

This press release cheat allowed the TV guestpert to do the producer's job and get her story across.

The One-Sheet
Our producer friend, Joe Scott, used a one-sheet instead of a press release in the Jackie Johnson story, as mentioned in chapter 2. This is also another sufficient substitute. A one-sheet is a fact sheet that provides all of the pertinent details to a particular story such as the who, what, where, when, how, why, and most important, who to contact.

CONTACT: Joe Scott, xxx-xxx-xxxx or email at xxx@xxx.com

**ARUBA CASE OF MISSING TEENAGER BEGS QUESTION
"CAN AMERICANS EXPECT THE SAME LEGAL RIGHTS WHEN
TRAVELING ABROAD DURING MISSING PERSONS CASES?"**

SPOKESPERSON: Jackie Johnson

WHY: Jackie Johnson's daughter, Erin, went missing while in Cabo San Lucas, Mexico, after a fight with her American boyfriend.

WHAT HAPPENED: Erin's body was found strangled and burned and her boyfriend was set free with no formal criminal investigative follow-up by Mexican authorities.

WHEN: Date of Erin Johnson's disappearance: April 28, 2001

AVAILABLE FOR INTERVIEWS

###

So far, you've had to capture your essence in a bio, wrap your pitch or hook up in a press release, and fold it all up in a folder that reflects the spirit of what you want to get across to television producers so they will give you access to that almighty audience on the other side of that TV screen.

Producing Your Tape or Reel

It is an absolute necessity to have a demo tape or reel as a tool in your press kit. Producers don't take chances on talent unless they can see what you look like on camera. Those of you who have not yet found your way onto TV or even local cable access programs (see chapter 4), fear not! You do need a show reel, but I know how to make one for you newbies. Keep reading...

If you get nothing else out of this book, heed the following information. I have sat in casting sessions and guest searches where hundreds of demo reels were submitted, and I can tell you that when it comes down to it, you should impress them with who you want to be, not who you were.

Meaning...what? The old way of making a show reel of your clips is to place your most recent appearances first, followed in reverse chronological order (newest to oldest) with the rest of your TV spots. But a popular show should outrank lesser shows, so don't put a local news clip before your big *Ricki Lake* segment just because it is more recent. Popularity sells!

The New Way to Reel

"But wait, Jacquie," you may be thinking and/or saying out loud, "you said this was the old way of making show reels. What's the new way?" I am very glad you asked me that question, true believers!

The *Get on TV* philosophy takes a twenty-first-century view of show reels. Here's the inside line:

> Your show reel is your movie trailer.

Again, it needs to reflect the job or show you *want,* not the job or show you've already had. The first thirty seconds of your reel should highlight your essence. In fact, I don't even need to hear you speak in the first thirty seconds. Let me see the images of you accompanied by some really great music.

Why take such a seemingly flashy approach? *To keep a producer or casting agent watching your tape.* With the old way of producing your reel, if the producer doesn't like your look or what you say, then it's *eject.* Maybe your best stuff would have been next up, but who will ever see it? With the new way of editing your reel, the first thirty seconds should play like a movie trailer with quick cuts, cool music, and flashy images, all capturing the essence of you.

Computer editing is now available for home computers at an afford-able price, and even you small-town denizens should have access to pro-fessionals with such equipment. For example, most professional wedding videographers will know how to cut your reel from a technical stand-point. So if the idea of editing makes you nervous—and the process is not as simple as it may sound—seek professional help. Even businesses like Kinko's offer basic editing services.

This new, next-generation show reel is especially great for new talent who have never had an official television appearance (worried newbies, this means you!). You've all seen home movie reels or *America's Funniest Home Video* shows. You get the gist. Your reel need not be a Steven Spielberg production. Just concentrate in the image you want to project.

After the thirty seconds of images and music, then go verbal. Newbies, be creative. Try the "ten questions" exercise from the last section. *Do not* just let the camera roll for ten minutes as you churn through the Q&A. This material needs to be whittled down via editing to sound bites, small, quotable lines of dialogue that reflect your hook, pitch, and field of expertise. Again, think of this as a movie trailer. Keep moving forward. Do not linger. Do not include dead air, such as pauses for reflection.

Those of you who already have television segments to your credit will use clips from your appearances here. I stress the word "clip." You may have been the sole focus of a five minute segment on *Oprah*, but only use the introduction and the highlights. Whole segments are *out*; short, user-friendly edited clips are *in*. The only thing you are trying to impress upon the producer here is "I've been booked on *Oprah* and this is how smart I am"—with a sharp sound bite.

TRT = Total Running Time

The TRT of your reel should be between two and a half minutes and five minutes. *No longer.* Did you hear me? No. Longer. Laugh now, but when you are trying to get your reel down from twelve minutes to two—it's a tough task, indeed. Cutting down the material you've worked so hard to accumulate feels like *Sophie's Choice,* but you *have* to do so. No matter how fascinating you or your story are, *nobody* will sit through a too-long show reel. We the producers have ADD. Get our attention. Show us what you need us to know about you, and get out of there.

Include Your Contact Info

What's the first thing most parents do when they send their two- and three-year-olds off for that first day in preschool? They write the child's name on *everything*, from lunchboxes and spoons to socks and shoes. In a bustling and often downright hectic production office, materials have a way of going astray and getting lost. Your reel and contact number is no exception!

Your name and phone number need to be added to "slates" at the reel's beginning and end, not just the exterior spine of the tape. If you have access to a PC or Mac home editing system, the "Help" menu will tell you how to add such "titles." Your friendly neighborhood wedding videographer or Kinko's clerk will be able to execute this requirement with ease.

Why is this "insurance" step necessary? Because tape slipcases can get separated from the tapes themselves. Tapes get banged around. And more often than not, the press kits are separated from the demo tapes. It's easier to store the tapes separately from the kits in an office space. Tape and press kit trafficking can be intense and constant. Don't get lost in the shuffle!

Presentation of Materials

Due to my extensive experience both as a producer and media consultant, I was recently invited to participate in a casting session for a NBC prime-time reality show. The production company was looking for the next Jeff Probst, the star host of *Survivor*. We received no less than one thousand tapes after the breakdowns (demographic profile: age, gender, etc.) were announced. Every talent agency, every manager, every entertainment lawyer in town, sent us their clients' show reels. Individuals without representation got into the game too: determined people just like you.

To my great surprise, some of the sloppiest submissions came from top talent agencies. In fact, if I were a client of some of these industry giants,

I'd be extremely disappointed to learn that my business was being handled in such an unprofessional manner.

It was a small boutique agency that impressed me the most: Ken Linder and Associates. They'd obviously put considerable thought into how their client's submissions should be handled, and this attention to detail and presentation separated them from the pack. Every show reel came in the agency's distinctive green slipcases, with the client's bios and headshots rubberbanded around the tape cassette. That way, the risk of tape and materials being separated was reduced. Every client's bio was neatly printed on the company's customized stationery, and each tape had the company's slate at the beginning followed by the talent's details. Lastly, every tape was a clean copy, and not a "muddy" dub of a dub of a dub. If you thought that the major agencies would give their clients such professional treatment, you'd be wrong indeed. That's why I am here to tell you that do-it-yourself can get you on TV.

> ## *DUB*
>
> A copy of a tape source.

Out of those thousand show reel submissions, Ken Linder and Associates' tapes had the best chance of being noticed based on the quality of presentation alone. You see, it's not just what's been popped in the VCR that counts. A producer is not just functioning "in the moment" and fulfilling casting or booking requirements, they're also filing away guests and talent that they *can't* currently use. The whole casting experience can be grueling, so the submissions that make our jobs more pleasant or entertaining, or make us feel like you really care about the process, are the ones that we'll be most inclined to call right away or call to mind at a later date on another project. So it bears repeating again:

Presentation counts.
Be prepared.

Returning Materials

There's a simple rule for the return of materials. Wanna know what it is? Things *never ever* get returned. Send copies only. It's extremely unfair to invite a busy show producer to look at your materials and then expect us to return them to you. Besides, you want your materials passed around and shared, not borrowed and returned. This has happened to me on numerous occasions. I've even had people call me six months after a submission and say, "I sent you something last fall, could you please return it to me now." I'm like, "Huh? Oh, you want my busy intern to comb through the *hundreds* of press kits and show reels that we carefully save and categorize according to shape, color, and entertainment value." Our offices are not spacious. Once we've passed on your material or had you on a show, we throw them all away. And yes, some of us even recycle...

Sending Materials

There is a strategy to sending materials to producers. First off, you've put a lot of time and energy into your press kits and demo reels and you want them to reach the hands of your intended producers. Here are a few things you will want to know.

Originals: Handle with Care—Not!

You wouldn't send a priceless family heirloom through the mail, would you? Then why do people often send original, one-of-a-kind items to producers?

Remember our kind gentleman from my seminar who survived the Holocaust? If his poorly wrapped package had been sent to a mailroom with more stringent rules as to suspicious packages, the original family photos he enclosed would have been lost for all time. Nowadays, there is no excuse not to have photographs copied or VHS tapes dubbed.

We've all seen news images of families left homeless by fires (particularly us Californians!). Time and again, we note that the ones who are the most upset are the folks who did not have the time to save the family photographs. Insurance can replace the contents of a home, but not the memories immortalized in snapshots.

Here is an anecdote that illustrates the dangers of trusting originals to even the most careful and well-intentioned person or company:

A production company was producing a TV biography about a movie star. They were sent the star's original childhood photos and promised to treat them with absolute, all-encompassing care. What they did not count on was an out-of-the-blue "act of God." A freak fire erupted in the building and spread to the company's editing bay. The photos were incinerated. Some of them had been digitally scanned and transferred into the company's Avid Editing Systems (essentially, fancy PCs) in preparation for placement in the documentary. But the photos that had not been copied were irretrievably lost. The company and the network have a six-figure lawsuit pending against them for loss and damage to the original photos.

I can only go on record here for myself, but I promise you that I am marching in step with my industry. *I assume no responsibility for original materials that are sent to me.*

Shipping Methods

I understand and applaud the value of thriftiness. I know that some of you may be on very tight budgets. But in regard to shipping your materials, I strongly urge you to use priority mail rather than regular mail if you want them to be seen.

I send all of my materials through priority mail, because when I receive priority mail at work, I know it's important. Sending your materials overnight or via priority mail make them stand out. The package may sit in a corner for a day or two, but my staff and I will know that it's special. We'll open these packages first, then the regular mail submissions.

Want to get to the head of the line? Want to be the early-bird submission? Then you'll send it with care, via FedEx, USPS Priority Mail, or any other widely used service. Think of it as dressing for success, only it's the mail that's looking spiffy and important, not you yourself!

CD-ROMs

If we seek to impress with FedEx, shouldn't we also try to impress with the latest technology? It seems logical, doesn't it? But the practical answer is a resounding, nay, a thundering NO!

As far as CD-ROMs go, they're *supposed* to play on multiple computers, but here's a news flash: sometimes they don't. Maybe the formats or applications are not right. How much do you know about the compatibility of Windows Media Player or Quick Time? Can you factor Macs into your equation? Then again, maybe all that stuff is A-Okay, but maybe a producer or intern just can't get them to play because they are not computer-savvy. If you send along a CD-ROM that is guaranteed to play on a computer in the Betelgeuse star system but if it fails to play here on Earth, it's going in the garbage.

VHS or DVD?

Well, what about burning a DVD then? Everybody has a DVD player these days, right? Well on that last count, you may well be right. Producers and their staff probably do have DVD players...in their own homes! Television is an expensive medium. Production office expenses are considered below-the-line costs, which mean that all pretenses towards luxury go out the window. Furniture is rented, and often not only unstylish, but rather shabby. VCR players are cheap and plentiful, new and used. Why buy a DVD player when it A) costs a little more, and B) 99 percent of show reel submissions are VHS tapes? Television production offices will catch up with technology, but for the foreseeable future, assume Stone Age levels of sophistication. Send VHS tapes, not DVDs.

Here is a DVD-related horror story. It's not horrible for me, but rather for the person who submitted the item. I received a DVD show reel from an editor who was looking for work. And I was indeed scouting for a new editor. But when I popped his DVD into my player, I could not for the life of me get past the opening menu selection screen! I never saw his work and he did not get the job.

The bottom line is this: it can be frustrating to figure out somebody else's technology. Play by the rules and just send VHS!

Audio

There are many occasions where a well meaning candidate sends a CD or cassette of their radio appearances because they haven't had the opportunity to appear on television yet.

I'm sympathetic to this situation. I know that you want to make the transition to television. But sending audio materials is another big no-no! Television is a visual medium. Listening to an audiotape of your radio appearance, even if the subject was riveting or you were absolutely hilarious, tells me nothing about your suitability for TV. Potential TV guest-perts must communicate in the medium they want to be exposed on.

Email or Snail Mail

It is my experience that sending your materials by email is not effective. Major Internet service providers such as the mighty AOL (America Online) automatically compress (a form of translation) certain email file attachments, and if I lack the right decompression software, your materials will not get a look.

Some producers do like working with email. But there is a protocol involved here, even if you only wish to send a "meet and greet" email message. Don't send email unless you are invited to do so. It is impolite to send unsolicited emails to a producer. Some producers find this uncomfortably reminiscent of a stalker's tricks. At best, it's like telemarketing! So I will not be impressed if you finagled my work email somehow. I know that none of my staff would have given it out to just anybody who asks for it. This is standard operating procedure in any business.

Following Up

So you've sent in your press kit and show reel. And then you hear nothing, so you may call us and say *"I know you're really busy, but have you had a chance to look at my materials?"* Most likely, we will not know who you are or where your materials are at that very moment. So we say *"Can you check back in a few weeks?"* Then six weeks pass like molasses and you politely call us back once again. But we still haven't watched your reel or seen your press kit. We will most likely be somewhat apologetic, as we know you're looking forward to good news.

What do you do next? That's easy! Go to chapter 7 for advice on how to be persistent without being annoying, and when to call it quits and move on to the next show submission.

The most exciting part of having a finished press kit is knowing that the other work—the hook, pitch, and platform—is concrete enough to put into these material terms for your sale to a producer. If you can do this, I assure you, the rest of the journey gets much easier.

TV GUESTPERT: CHECKLIST

- Does your press kit reflect your branding and encompass your mission statement?
- Does your bio, reel, headshot exemplify your essence?
- Is your contact information clearly marked on all parts of your press kit?
- Does your pitch translate well into the contents of your press kit?

Chapter 6

Space: The Final Frontier...What Show Is Right for You?

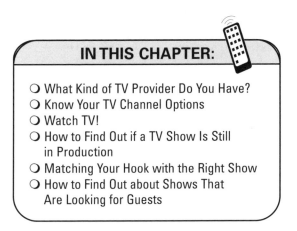

IN THIS CHAPTER:

- ○ What Kind of TV Provider Do You Have?
- ○ Know Your TV Channel Options
- ○ Watch TV!
- ○ How to Find Out if a TV Show Is Still in Production
- ○ Matching Your Hook with the Right Show
- ○ How to Find Out about Shows That Are Looking for Guests

All right, people. I know you're excited and want to get down to the business of getting booked as soon as possible. But while you may be eager to make a trip, journey, or voyage, you have to know what the options are in order to maximize your potential experience. There are places that you have always wanted to visit, but there are probably even more locations of which you may be unaware. This chapter is a guide to all the places you can go; a map that shows the general terrain.

You've developed pitches, hooks, and mission statements, and are now ready to go out into the big wide world and spread your message, story, ideas, opinions, and/or expertise. But what about those of you who have not been able to keep up with the scores of TV shows and network outlets that are out there? You know many names on the hit parade, sure—*Oprah, Maury, Montel, Today, Entertainment Tonight*—all the usual suspects. But you guys need to cast your net as wide as possible to haul in bookings. Most of you will have to begin on the fringes, far from the light of major ratings and audiences, and work your way inward to the mainstream.

This chapter is not just about finding cool "locations" on the map of television's terrain. You also have to know if you are compatible with your target destinations. It's time to match your pitch and hooks with a show that is right for you.

Exciting, isn't it? And sort of like *The Dating Game*...

What Kind of TV Provider Do You Have?

Let's begin with the very basics. In order to determine what show is right for you, we first want to know what kind of service provider it is that brings television programming to your home. If you don't know what you may be missing as far as access and targeting goes (what? You didn't know there was a network about X?), it's a little like trying to write a book, but not realizing that the alphabet goes beyond the letter Q. If you don't know that there are useful options beyond Q, then your words and your ability to communicate are limited.

Know Your TV Channel Options

By understanding what kind of service you have or don't have, you will see whether or not you are viewing the full range of television appearance opportunities.

TV PROVIDERS

Old-fashioned "rabbit ears"
Rooftop antenna
Cable
Satellite receiver

Rabbit Ears

"Rabbit ears" are those small antennas that sit atop the TV. You know, the ones you have to fiddle with while the most exciting moment of the Super Bowl is going down? They act in tandem with the television's built-in apparatus and pick up broadcasted TV signals. But if this is what you have, your access to programming is limited. You really need to consider expanding your options (or hang out with your neighbors more).

Antenna

A rooftop antenna extends the range of your TV. Here, you may be able to pick up broadcasts from other cities nearby, depending on the strength of their signals. But this option is also limiting to your goals. There are, quite literally, *hundreds* of television shows that you will be unaware of that are not broadcast "through the air" in what we used to think of as the conventional way.

Cable

The next step up is cable TV. Cable service providers differ from company to company, and often from region to region. Adelphia in the Midwest may not offer the same networks as Adelphia on the West Coast. These service providers decide what networks they will carry according to licensing fees. They have to pay for the right to carry ESPN or PAX.

For years, a young neighbor of mine complained because her provider carried MTV, one of the most popular networks, but not the new MTV2 sister channel. She wanted to direct music videos, and MTV had switched away from a video format towards game shows and reality shows like *Real World*. Amazingly enough, MTV did not play many videos at all. That was why the network created MTV2, which is all videos, all the time. My neighbor's ability to study music videos and learn this market suffered for her lack of access. She danced a jig when her cable service finally picked up MTV2, although it was part of an additional package of networks.

If you have a basic cable package, you are still limiting your options. Many of us are on tight budgets, but it will be well worth the investment to order a fuller cable TV package for a few months while you do your research. Just make sure you don't commit to long-range package contracts with expensive cancellation fees! This isn't indulgence, this is homework, folks. Study up!

Satellite

Satellite service providers like DirectTV have been gaining major inroads over the last fifteen years. They too offer a wide array of packages, in addition to pay-per-view movies and events, which do not relate to our purposes and goals. It's amazing how much programming a satellite in space can beam directly into your home through a small rooftop dish. To those of us above the age of twenty, satellite TV may seem very Space Age indeed.

To add to the complexity of choice, new cable and satellite networks launch all the time. For instance, The Horror Channel is gearing up for business: all horror, all the time. Of course, like the SciFi Channel, it will eventually get around to creating reality TV programming and game shows to suit its unique audience. So that's a channel to keep in mind for developing those Halloween hooks!

The lesson here is that you need to do your homework and know the terrain of television in all its diverse glory. If you do not develop a list of fifty shows you may be suitable for pitching to, you will soon run out of options when they say, "Try us again another time." The more targets you aim for, the more hits (and eventually bull's-eyes) you will receive.

Watch TV!

Watch TV! Sounds simple, but this is true! Many of us are too busy to watch TV, yet how can we be on it if we don't see it? While trying to get on TV, we must become consumers of the relevant television programming.

If studying network outlets is getting to know the terrain of "TV Land," then observing individual shows is like mastering a specific city map. Apply the lessons from this book, study each show with diligence, and you'll know everything from mountains and valleys, down to street corners and intersections.

It's a great idea to videotape the shows you watch. Often patterns only become apparent if you take another, more measured look. The rewind button will be a major boom towards understanding the way a show is structured, or the kind of questions a particular host asks. A host's craft and skill are meant to be invisible: the illusion of spontaneity is what a show shoots for. But every host is a professional, and if you study their "moves" you'll gain insights that will help you custom design your hooks and press kit materials for specific shows.

What to look for:

- *Get to know a show's style or content pattern.* This is important to determine the flavor of matching your hook to the show. For example, does the show only do celebrity segments on Fridays?
- *Do they use the same guest on the same subject matter?* Are they already using a featured TV guestpert for your particular topic? If so, how will you offer yourself to the show that will make it unique and different than the guestpert they are currently using? Can you be a TV guestpert in the same segment that they currently use a TV guestpert for already?
- *Have they covered your topic?* If your message is "Dogs wouldn't maul people if people knew how to handle dogs" and they've been covering a news story on this topic, what can you do to make your hook work for their audience?
- *Is your idea even suitable for their content?* Oh, come on, Las Vegas

showgirls between 7 a.m. and 8 a.m. won't work on the *Today Show* because the kids haven't gone to school yet.

- *What is the common thread of the show?* Just like I've been asking you, what is the hook of that show and how can your hook match up with it?

I've heard colleagues complain time and time again. Someone calls them to pitch a show idea and it immediately becomes apparent that this person has never even watched the show! I've even had professional publicity agents pitch on behalf of clients that are unsuited to what I'm doing. So if you think that you can wing it, that there seems to be no difference between *Montel* and *Maury*, think again. Pitching irrelevant material to a producer will only make you seem unprepared and even foolish. That producer may be inclined to blow off your next submission volley. If you were a hot stockbroker, how long would you keep your success ratio if you kept cold-calling uncomprehending ten year olds? You'd soon be out on the street selling hot dogs.

> Bottom line: *Know the market, know the show.*

I cannot stress how important this is. I deal with ill-prepared pitchers on every show I work on. Not that I'm above making an error in judgment myself...

Here is an anecdote that still makes me blush with embarrassment. An *LA Times* columnist called me out of the blue one day. He was interested in learning more about my media consultancy business for a potential column item he was writing. The *LA Times* is a major paper, with national distribution: talk about a great opportunity!

The meeting was to take place right away. I agreed, eager to see my name and my business profile in print. But, my dear and faithful readers, I did not do my homework and I flunked the assignment. I did buy an *LA Times* on the way to the meeting to get the Cliff's Notes version of his work, but guess what? This journalist's column appears on different days. So I had no idea what kind of writer he was. Breezy and hip, or sober and detail oriented? I had no clue.

Thinking that I could rely on charm and just wing the meeting, I showed up and made an ass out of myself. It was an awkward meeting for me. He probably thought that I was not taking him seriously, or, worse yet, that I was not serious about what I did. Both these perceptions were as far from the truth of the matter as can be. But I had conveyed a poor impression.

Needless to say, I never made it into his column, and he was polite enough not to slam me in print! This story still makes me squirm with shame. I had blown the opportunity to wow somebody with my well-prepared confidence and disrespected a fellow professional. Don't get caught unprepared!

Included for your review is the A to Z of television networks. This list includes the outlets of which most shows or programs live. The list (see Appendix: The Big List) lists all the homes on TV. Get to know each of the networks like a new neighborhood to see all the possibilities there are for show outlets. To be clear, this is a list of networks—major and cable—not a list of television shows. Parked at each of these networks is a multiplicity of programs for your review. Have fun exploring!

How to Find Out if a TV Show Is Still in Production

Let's assume that you've mastered your new job as a consumer and analyst of television programming. You know exactly what shows you're right for, and exactly who to contact. There's another potential bump in the road ahead. It is possible that a show you have targeted is on hiatus or has even been cancelled. *A show that is on hiatus is temporarily out of production.* This could happen for a variety of reasons: 1) the production of the show is simply on "summer vacation." Shows like *Dr. Phil* take the summer off. 2) A show may have fulfilled its contractual obligations to a network and finished taping the agreed upon number of episodes, and the network executives may still be deciding whether or not to purchase another slate or season of shows.

That's right, you can study a show for two or three months, but everybody working on it may have been fired, or may not be back in the office for weeks on end, or may not know if they have a job to come back to.

So you need to know if a show is in production, which means that it is actively "in session," seeking guests, and making shows.

> Not in Production: a show that is *not in production* is no longer being produced or made. Literally, there is no one answering phones. There is no office. The staff has gone on to other jobs, even if you are still seeing it air on TV.

There are several different ways to find out. Contact your local service provider to ask them for the contact information for the network that runs the show of interest to you. If you have been following my advice, you will already know how to contact the network thanks to our handy *Get on TV* list of television networks. But if it's a new network that's not on the list, then try your service provider.

Once you get through to the network, ask the operator if the show is in production, and if so, who is producing it? Sometimes the network will produce the show in house sometimes it's through an independent production company. Of course, see if the show has a website and try contacting them directly.

Matching Your Hook with the Right Show

There are three key factors to consider when matching your hook to the right show.

First, your hook itself.

Second, *timeliness*.

Third, the show's format.

1. Your Hook

As I've stated before, not every hook will work on every show. The important thing in applying your hook is to determine what show is right for you. I worked as a senior producer on the TV show *Men Are from Mars, Women Are from Venus,* based upon John Gray's best-selling book. The show's slant is that all hooks had to represent the man's point of view versus a woman's point of view.

As a producer, I took the concept of "emotional eating" and produced a segment on the differences between how men and women relate to food based on their emotional states. Celebrity nutritionist and author Cheryl Sindell was my expert guest of choice. An informative piece about the issue alone would have failed to match the show's given slant and style. I had to gear the segment toward the man versus women format. This constraint sometimes worked as a crutch, making it easy to reject topics that did not fit into the format. But at the same time, this dynamic was also an impediment to the program's variety. Due to the specific focus of the show, which was more rigorous than most talk TV programs, it was more of a challenge to book guests.

Apply the same technique to shows such as *The View,* which features a round table panel of female hosts, or to *The Daily Show,* which features topics from a comically exaggerated current event point-of-view. When watching *The View,* there is a distinct point-of-view (thus the name) that the panel of women take on subjects they cover which is distinctly different than the way Jon Stewart covers a subject, yet the same subject can end up on both shows. The spin would be fundamentally different.

FORMULA

Hook + Timeliness + Show Format = Pitch

Case Study: The Andrea Yates News Hook

Several years ago, Texas mother of five Andrea Yates, suffering from an acute case of postpartum depression, took the lives of her children. It shocked the nation and divided us on the "insanity defense" issue. We had a client who acts as an expert trial witness on behalf of the defendants in these controversial and tragic murder cases.

When we pitched my client to the national media outlets, we didn't take the obvious hooks "Why did this woman kill her children?" or "Is Yates guilty or insane?" Our hook was as follows—"90 percent of mothers who murder their children are on some form of antidepressants." We could back up this statement with solid research from the International Coalition of Drug Awareness. The hook clearly implies that drugs like Prozac can have disastrous side effects. And since we all know somebody who has used antidepressants at some time, it had irresistible appeal that demanded attention.

That hook took care of national pitches. But we wanted to hit our local South California news markets as well. This was an important message: people needed to understand that antidepressants were potentially lethal and destructive. We needed to craft a hook that tied into the concerns of the Los Angeles area. The Phil Hartman murder-suicide case in which his wife, who used major antidepressants, shot him dead, killed herself, and left her two children orphans, strongly suggested a medication-based correlation between the two tragedies.

Our ability to craft show and format specific hooks enabled us to relate the Andrea Yates story to events in our own backyard. What you should take away from this is the necessity to recraft those hooks and attach them to shows that are right for you. Find a way of meshing, or fitting into a show's vibe, format or style. There may not be an "in," but by being creative, you expand your booking potential. Incidentally, Andrea Yates's case was overturned, which brings us to our next point...

2. Timeliness

Timeliness is also important in determining how your hook can be recrafted or modified to fit in with a given show. Internally, a television show's staff is issued a show grid, a calendar line-up of the upcoming content. Even in news programs, where content is always changing every hour of the day, segments are still roughly sketched out and planned according to a calendar of events. Your local newscast may be taping Christmas segments in July.

If and when your hook coincides with a holiday (Labor Day, Halloween, etc.) or anniversary (ten years since the OJ verdict), then give yourself about six weeks of lead time—an insider's rule of thumb—to get yourself out there, because the shows are well into the making of their programming regardless of whether they are live or taped. In other words, even though Valentine's Day is almost two months away, they may be taping their Heart's Day program segments at the end of December.

If you were to take our expert trial witness from the previous example and update that hook with some timely relevance, then you could use the recent Tom Cruise/Matt Lauer discussion from the *Today* show about pharmaceuticals as the new hook and then match it appropriately to a suitable show format.

3. Show Formats

There are several different types of show formats. The biggest distinction that needs to be made is between scripted and unscripted programming. By now, you probably understand that this book is dealing with what is referred to in the industry as "unscripted" programming. Although, technically, it's not at all "unscripted," but in comparison to sitcoms and dramas which are literally "scripted" programs, then the following would be considered unscripted. Listed below are the various types of "unscripted" programming formats.

National News: 6 p.m. national news; *World News Tonight*
Pitch: Serious news with national relevance and importance.
Local News: Eyewitness News
Pitch: Must have local or regional relevance to the community.
Talk: From *Oprah* to *Jerry Springer* to *Ellen*
Pitch: Must have a hook that matches the personality of the show and be relevant to a female daytime audience.
Magazine: Entertainment Tonight, Access Hollywood, Extra
Pitch: Should have a celebrity angle.

Morning News Shows: The Today Show, The Early Show

Pitch: Must be informationally driven, but with a lighter spin than the national news, and be considered appropriately for morning or for national.

Reality: Survivor, The Osbournes, The Real World

Pitch: Would be varietal, based on the circumstances of the story line.

News Magazines: Dateline, 60 Minutes, 48 Hrs

Pitch: Often investigative.

Documentary: National Geographic Explorer

Pitch: Geared toward the genre of the individual show (e.g., animals, space, automobiles)

News-Talk: Catherine Crier; *Hannity and Colmes*

Pitch: Current events or political.

Lifestyle: Trading Spaces

Pitch: Expertise crafted around the individual show (e.g., design, crafts, fashion).

Game: Jeopardy, Hollywood Squares

Pitch: Craft a hook around a pop culture question or around a potential prize giveaway.

Clearly understanding a show's format will help you choose which hook to apply when getting ready to do a pitch. Remember the "Andrea Yates/antidepressant" pitch? We used the same pitch with different hooks to land spots on two different formats: national and local news. We could have created still more hooks to make the pitch appropriate for formats ranging from Talk, to Documentary to News-Talk.

At the end of the day, it is your creativity and ingenuity in regards to crafting hooks that will land you on TV.

How to Find Out about Shows That Are Looking for Guests

Print

As television producers, when we are looking for talent, guests, people, or stories, we often put ads in local newspapers. Ads from us can also be found in the pages of *Backstage, Backstage West; The Hollywood Reporter,* or *Variety.* You can get hard copy or Internet subscriptions to these periodicals, or try looking for them at your local library. So it pays, as always, to read the "fine print!"

Internet

I was once involved in a project for Think Huge Productions called *Fanography,* which airs on MTV. We were searching for real-life Limp Bizkit fans to tell the history of the rock band. Our search was relatively easy. Where better to look for fans of the band than on its official website? We contacted fans in chat rooms, and also did the same on the most popular or interesting unofficial (fan-designed and operated) websites.

NEWS FLASH

Many networks and TV shows have their own websites, which regularly post guest searches or casting calls. Don't rely on these searches alone: consider them one of many tools in your arsenal.

More casually, you might try Craigslist.org, a popular website for TV postings of all shapes and sizes, from casting calls to job openings. BreakdownServices.com is a listing used by agents and managers that television producers post listings on. It is a subscriber service: if you want to browse, you have to pay a fee. Check it out at least for a limited time to get an idea of what we're looking for.

Again, if you want to get on a reality show like *Survivor* or *Blind Date,* apply the same research approach to tracking down the production company. Call the office to see when they will be casting or holding auditions again. For example, *The Real World* usually announces casting via short commercial spots on the show itself as the most recent season ends.

This may seem obvious to many, but we do get asked about it so much that it bears mentioning. If a show or production company has an open audition and it's not in your city, no, they will not and cannot pay for your transportation! If you miss out, do not despair, for many shows have nationwide casting calls in which you can send in your audition tape. More on reality TV in chapter 11.

Start Local

Don't feel overwhelmed by all these outlets and formats and options and variable hooks. You don't have to tackle them all at once. Start slow, start local.

Your local ten o'clock morning news is a great place to start. I also suggest going into other nearby markets. If you are in Vegas, try Los Angeles, San Diego, or Phoenix—markets that are local enough that you can readily become familiar with them. There's the "visitor from out of town" factor in action. For various reasons, you may receive more attention if you are "just in town for a few days" rather than banging on your own door, so to speak.

Think of the local beat as a grassroots approach to getting booked for the big leagues. Think globally, act locally. The Spokane 10 a.m. news show can be your stepping-stone to the national show you know you're just right for.

The really great news is that there are many show possibilities. I suppose the way I think of it is that if you were going to different parties in your neighborhood, you would dress based on the theme, the time of day, and who was giving the party and you would bring an appropriate dish based on that information. Finding the right show is like determining the right outfit and the right dish to bring that would be appropriate to that particular party that you are going to attend...and at each party you get to be the honored TV guestpert.

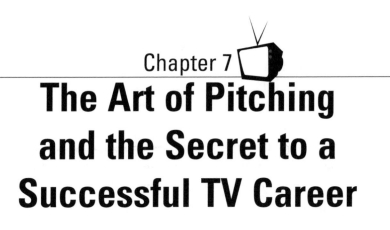

Chapter 7

The Art of Pitching and the Secret to a Successful TV Career

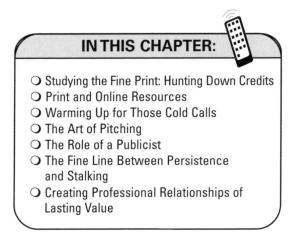

IN THIS CHAPTER:

- ○ Studying the Fine Print: Hunting Down Credits
- ○ Print and Online Resources
- ○ Warming Up for Those Cold Calls
- ○ The Art of Pitching
- ○ The Role of a Publicist
- ○ The Fine Line Between Persistence and Stalking
- ○ Creating Professional Relationships of Lasting Value

Studying the Fine Print: Hunting Down Credits

A show's credits reveal all! They tell you that elusive name you're so desperately looking for so that you can make that difficult cold call to a production office. There are so many gatekeepers in any given show's production office, that you need to know *exactly* who to target by name and professional title. If you try to bluff your way into a submission or a pitch, you will inevitably get cut out. And if a producer realizes that you have no clear idea what their show is about, they will be disinclined to book you. I'll say it yet again: *be prepared.*

In chapter 2 we covered the different titles and roles that exist within a television show's hierarchy. You may have visions of segment producers, associate producers, and bookers dancing in your head, but can you put a name to these positions? Now that you know *Who's Who,* it's time to focus on *Who's Where...*

The overall answer is simple: *credits* will tell you everything you need to know about those many "who's" you are about to seek out and communicate with. There are four primary methods of getting access to a show's all important credit information: the program's graphical "blink and you'll miss them" *end credits,* the show (or network's) *website,* certain industry focused *periodicals,* and various subscription service *websites,* which can provide you with a record of all the shows a particular producer has worked on in their career.

End Credits

You'd probably have to be a speed reading world class court stenographer with hawk-like 20/20 vision in order to absorb a television show's end credits as they zoom past. Why are they so rapid? Because if they played out like movie credits, the show in question would lose several minutes of air time. And how many of you stay to the end of a movie's credits, anyway?

The easiest way to collect end credit information to get a producer's name is the most obvious: videotape the show and play it back at your leisure. For thoroughness's sake, I'd advise you to transcribe *all* the producing credits for each show, as well as brief notations as to what each segment was about. That way you don't have to go back to your tape library and fast forward to the end of the show in question should you decide to pitch fresh hooks to a different segment producer who might be a better target for the new material.

As far as credit-tracking goes, TiVo is also an excellent resource. You can record shows without setting up your VCR or even being at home to watch them. TiVo also enables you to play a show back at a slow speed, as well as freeze frame those whizzing end credits. TiVo is also a key resource if you plan to check out and follow a wide array of shows that are appropriate for your goals.

There is one important thing to remember about end credits: they often do not list the show's entire production staff. The crew heads usually get the full treatment, but a producer may only be credited if they worked on that particular show. In this way, a show's end credits vary from day to day, and do not necessarily indicate every possible avenue of submission for you.

And what about production credits for local radio programming? Just call up the station and ask for details. You should also try talking to the station's program director and ask specific questions about a show's format and content.

Print and Online Resources

I recommend *RTIR* (*Radio-TV Interview Report*) to my clients. It's a producer-targeted trade publication with wide distribution in the USA and Canada (an added plus). Published three times a month, each issue lists available guests, experts, and authors who are available for live and in-studio interviews. It's a great way to get your name and profile out there, but it works best for individuals who have already built a solid media platform. You have to pay for the subscription as well as a listing fee.

Online resources are many and varied. Some are professional, while others are wannabe sites and services that will not provide you with worthwhile services. So do your research and satisfy yourself as to what any given company is promising.

WWW.TVGUESTPERT.COM

As a result of this publishing, many TV guests and clients have asked how I could support them. As a result, tvguestpert.com has been launched. This is an Internet database for producers to search for professional TV guests or experts like yourself where you can post your bio, press clippings, and demo reels, but we screen heavily, so make sure you are prepared.

Other reliable subscriber online resources are:

Bulldog Reporter's Media Relations HQ (www.infocomgroup.com), which is mainly for PR professionals, but does offer an array of media list services (such as producer's names and addresses).

IMDBPro (www.imdbpro.com) is a service of the free *Internet Movie Database* (www.imdb.com), that provides subscribers with information on any given television and movie professional. This is a great way of researching the career of a producer you wish to pitch to.

TVtracker.com specializes in tracking upcoming shows that are in development, but it also features a number of other resources, including credit listings to individual shows.

Warming Up for Those Cold Calls

Raise your hand if you've ever been filled with dread, indecision, or unease at the thought of asking somebody out on a date. It may not have happened since high school (lucky you!), but most of us can still identify with the attendant nerves and butterflies. It's an "easier said than done" situation. In theory, all one has to do is pick up the phone and call our object of affection, or confidently mosey up, open our mouths, start talking, and our true charming and winning selves will become instantly apparent. Ah, if only it was so easy! Often, the more we try to talk ourselves down from nervousness, the more anxious we become!

For many of us, the same can be said about *cold-calling,* which is the art of calling a person we have never seen or talked to before and asking for some sort of favor, whether a job interview, a charitable donation to a worthy cause, or the chance to tell them about a story, issue, or product pitch.

Cold-calling can be difficult, but as with many fields of endeavor, practice makes perfect, or at least much improved. That's all there is to it, really: practice. Write out three simple and central bullet points for your cold-call pitch. Remember the KISS rule: *Keep It Simple, Stupid!* You can get into details, selling points, and anecdotes *after* you have made the basic, up-front pitch.

Once you've composed your bullet points, practice by making imaginary cold calls. Talk to your bathroom mirror in the morning, pitch to your car as you drive to work, and then try your spiel out on family and friends. Note: you must beg them for frank honesty! If they try to spare your feelings, they are actually doing you a disservice. And for your part, you must learn to accept criticism, even if it is not quite constructive. Chances are that if a friend does not get your pitch, or thinks that it is boring, long-winded, or confusing, you may well need to polish it up. That negative reaction may be off-base or even outright wrong-headed but it does represent how a small fraction of listeners might perceive your performance. Don't scrap what you have if you get a negative reaction, but be honest with yourself and try to analyze if the naysayer has a point, even a point that you may disagree with. Remember the story of the emperor's new clothes: sometimes that lone voice of dissent may be more truthful than a chorus of kudos.

Navel-Gazing: Another Cautionary Tale

Before we plow on into the art of the pitch itself, we need to cover one more area of defensive pre-pitching strategy: navel-gazing.

No, *navel-gazing* does not refer to the semi-voyeuristic act of scoping out other people's exposed midriffs in public! It's a somewhat common term for not paying attention to what's going on outside of your own life and thoughts. If you get caught navel-gazing, you're contemplating your own belly button instead of looking out the window at life.

In ninth grade, my class had a class assignment to create a mythology story of our own devising, one that illustrated a lesson or warning. I labored hard and crafted a story that I was immensely proud of. It concerned a woman who was so vain that she spent all day gazing at her own reflection in the mirror, until her body wasted away to nothing, and her reflection was doomed to take on the aspect of whomever looked into that mirror. By thinking only of herself, she wound up losing herself.

I confess to being rather puffed up with pride over my elegant cautionary yarn, but to my shock I only received a B+ for work that I was absolutely sure warranted an A. Now, perhaps my syntax or spelling was to blame for the less-than-perfect mark. But years later, I discovered another possible reason as to why my teacher was not floored by my story: I had unwittingly repeated the Greek myth of Narcissus, in which a vain young man falls in love with his own reflection in a pool of water, losing real affection from Echo, a nymph who loved him. Echo pined away until only her voice remained, while Narcissus turned into the flower that bears his name to this day.

So my original idea wasn't so original: it was actually thousands of years old. I probably had heard the story at some point and forgotten it, who knows. The point is that what I believed to be a fresh and brand-new idea was no such thing. And after many years spent producing, during which time I must have heard tens of thousands of pitches, I can tell you that: A) there aren't that many original ideas out there, and B) sometimes new ideas occur simultaneously to different people because it exists in the zeitgeist.

As is the case with the art of storytelling, which some believe is based on endless variations on only eight basic plot scenarios, pitching is often a case of figuring out how to put old wine into new bottles. Recall how many new diet fads, books, and techniques debut year in and year out. The trick is how to make your diet plan (or anything you are pitching) sound fresh and intriguing. But you also need to be aware of the competition so you can avoid repeating those pitches, and that means doing a little research at the library, bookstore, or online.

And do not become discouraged if you discover that somebody else has already been a guest on your target TV show with a similar story, product, or specialty. This can actually be a positive thing, because it forces you to come up with new hooks for your material and it validates that you are on the right track with sellable ideas. *Necessity,* it is said, *is the mother of all invention.* If you really *want* something badly enough, you will find a way to do it. Once again, we return to one of our mantras: be prepared!

I'll leave you with this advice: if you keep your eyes only on the road ahead of you (your metaphorical navel!), you can wind up walking down a dead end or into a ravine, but if you keep your gaze fixed on the wider horizon, you will never lose sight of the direction you are headed in.

The Art of Pitching

I do believe that the art of pitching—making those cold calls, making that winning pitch, selling yourself as well as your story, product, or specialty—is literally an art. You either have the gift of the gab, or you do not. But while you may not be a Picasso or a Michelangelo, you can learn to be a really solid and dependable house painter. Diligent preparation and determination will get you across the finishing line time and time again.

Obviously, the more informed you are, the easier it is to make that pitch. Calling up a show's production office and asking, "Oh, does so-and-so still work there?" may well stir you up. If you sound unprepared, which equates with unprofessional, receptionists or junior staffers will do their best to politely *not* put you through to a producer, because truthfully, time is usually precious and in short supply. They won't want to put a person through who will then fumble their way through a conversation and a pitch. That situation is painful for everybody. Producers don't like anybody to feel uncomfortable because we know how hard it can be to cold call in any given situation.

Writer-producer Robert Kosberg is the author of *How to Sell Your Ideas to Hollywood* and *Pitching Hollywood: How to Sell Your TV and Movie Ideas*. He has taught a great many professional industry pitch seminars and is a successful reality television and movie producer. He says:

> You must have courage and conviction and belief in yourself. If you can get anyone on the phone from the secretary to the interns, and *briefly* explain who you are and that you have something terrific to offer to the company, you should get transferred to the next person up the ladder. I make calls convinced that I have something to offer.

I always research the company that I am about to call. I am always as informed as I can possibly be. Remember the name of everybody you speak with and see if they can help you. At very least, get information about what they are looking for. Even if the cold call results in making a thin connection, you want to create an opportunity to follow up.

For me, I've always listened to the pitches on the phone. Even if the pitch is not optimally presented, or repeats that of a prior booking, I *always* take down names and numbers because I've done this enough to know that I just may need you a week or a month later. I do my best not to blow anyone off and I feel that most of my colleagues do the same. In regards to those of you who may be nervous when cold-calling, remember that most producers will meet you halfway. The stereotype of impatient, cigar-chomping, demanding producers derives from the movie side of the entertainment industry. We TV folk are much more approachable, because we know that literally anybody may be the next "star of the week" on any given segment or program. Our success depends upon you!

The Nitty Gritty: How the Pitch Goes Down

Here is a bare bones, generic outline of the pitch process:

- You cold-call my show and ask to pitch to a specific producer.
- You are prepared, and so you get put through to me or one of my staff, whoever you have specifically targeted.
- You pitch your thing, baby! Keep it simple: just a few sentences.
- We ask you to send in your materials *only* if your pitch is compatible with our show's format and tone.
- You ask, "Can I call back and follow up?"
- We respond, "We'll let you know if we want to hear back from you."
- A week passes. You hear no word from us. At this point it is reasonable to assume that we *might* not have looked at your materials.
- You *can* call and follow up to inquire whether or not we have received your submission. Be specific and ask to speak to the producer

you have submitted to. Do not pressure in regards to our review of your materials. We'll get to it when we get to it.

- If we haven't received your materials or cannot presently find them if we have, *send the materials again.* Better safe than sorry.
- Follow up your follow-up call with a postcard query (or an airplane skywriting message, depending on your budget!).
- When six to eight weeks pass, it is time to *move on.* Your pitch is not happening.

Now, here's the thing: you can still keep pitching to us, provided that you come up with fresh hooks that relate to our format. Stay current with any new episodes of the show that have aired. If you are a promising guest candidate, we'll be glad to find a spot for you. This is not a pass/fail situation. Surprise us and reinvent yourself and the hooks into your content. If you stick with it, you may well get that sought-after and well-deserved booking.

According to Kosberg, "No never means no, but you can't be obnoxious. I don't get back to the same people who said no, but I will reapproach a no with a new and different hook. Your reputation counts. You don't want to be a stalker. You have to recognize common courtesy. If a person is absolutely adamant, then know when to let it go. Remember, your behavior reflects on a potential working relationship. If you turn off producers because you aren't a good listener, then why would they want to work with you?"

We, the producers, call that type of person *unproducible!*

COLD-CALLING

The act of calling somebody whom you do not know; this person in turn has no prior knowledge of who you are or why you are calling.

The Role of a Publicist

Some people simply cannot pitch themselves. They may be genius about creating their do-it-yourself marketing campaign and TV pitch, patient and effective in building their platform, confident on camera, but incapable of making an effective cold call that will get their foot in the door. Or others may not take or have the time that they need to create the relationships that are necessary to becoming a TV guestpert. The solution maybe to hire a publicist, aka public relations agent.

What does a publicist do? *The role of publicists is to gain exposure for their clients and to maintain the clients' image and branding.* Publicists do this by crafting effective press releases and creating attention-grabbing press kits. Television is one of many media avenues that publicists use to gain exposure for their clients.

In my world, publicists need producers to put their clients on TV. And producers need the clients of publicists to put on TV. While some publicists may have a Rolodex filled with producer and show contacts, others will have to utilize their professional skills to create these contacts on your behalf. In general, the greater a publicist's list of contacts are for your particular needs, the higher their fees will be. If you hire the PR version of Johnny Cochran, you'd best be prepared for a hefty bill of $2,500 to $10,000 a month. Don't expect less than six months to see results.

The important thing for you to remember is this: *a publicist does not get their client booked any faster than a person who is doing their own pitch publicity,* especially *if the pitch is not good.* In the end, it is all down to the pitch and the potential guest, as we have seen time and time again in this book.

And here's another reality that I'd like to share with you: *even if someone has a strong publicist, this does not make them any more legitimate than somebody handling their own pitching process.* So don't take out a second mortgage to pay for a high-priced publicity agent just to help land you a coveted spot on *The Chatty Cathy Show.* You don't necessarily *need* a publicist...speaking from my own experience, I have booked just as many, if not more, guests without a publicist than with a publicist. A good idea is a good idea, and a good guest with a good idea is what I am after...it doesn't matter who delivers it to me.

What a Publicist Provides

A publicist can offer any service that you've read so far in this book. Even if a publicist doesn't have any contacts, relationships, or history with the shows you may be targeting, they will still know exactly what to do to cultivate them. The media is their area of expertise. It is important to research potential publicists, or ask them precisely what their media experience is. You don't want somebody who has just set up shop, has never worked for an established firm, or can't foster your area of guest expertise. Don't be somebody's guinea pig!

A creative and experienced publicist will also be able to help you perfect your pitch, hooks, platforms, and mission statements, as well as devise an effective marketing strategy specially tailored to your needs. They will also school you in the do's and don'ts of media appearances (check out chapter 10 for a closer look at how you can prepare for and manage your own media appearances).

There's another potential upshot to having a publicist on your side. Some publicists or publicity firms have leverage. If I call them and I want something that they represent, like an established expert or famous guest, they might agree to hook me up in exchange for helping one of their newer or lesser clients with a booking. It can happen, but obviously such agencies are quite prestigious or influential. Otis the publicist from Saskatchewan may be bright and eager and professional, but unless I really, really, desperately need to book a Canadian dancing bear, he may not be able to cut a *quid pro quo* deal with me.

The leverage issue raises another point. While the majority of my booked guests either pitch themselves or are discovered by my diligent and resourceful staff, I do sometimes call publicists and put out feelers, i.e., "I'm looking for a doctor who can talk about this new weight loss study, do you have anybody?" Signing with a publicity agent can have this extra benefit.

It's important not to just sign on or contract with a PR firm without fully understanding the context within which they will view you as a client. You need to know if they have any other clients who overlap or duplicate your skill set, pitch, or product line. If the answer is no, then ask how they plan to publicize you as differentiated from another client. If the answer is yes, they do have a client just like you, then it is imperative that you understand how they plan to resolve any competition issues. How will they pitch two clients with the same profile to the pool of suitable shows? Who gets first dibs on *Oprah,* for instance? Will each client receive the same amount of attention from the publicity staff? Is there a "first come, first serve" principal in motion?

In a worst-case scenario (which should never happen), a publicity agent might sign you to nullify competition for their client-with-the-same-skill. This client gets top-tier attention, while you languish with the new agent with no experience. This is unlikely, but it pays to mentally prepare for any possibility. If something *can* happen, then it could happen to you. All you need to do to protect yourself, as is the case in most business situations, is to ask informed questions. And remember, if you decide to go with a publicist at this point in the book, then everything you have read up until this point should help you find the right publicist for you.

Time is money, so sometimes it is worth making an expenditure for a good publicist who will take on all of the time-consuming work of promoting you and your pitch. Publicists will get your name and pitch out there in the mediascape. They will hold your hand, give you pep talks, pick you up off the floor when your pitch falls flat at your favorite show, and rally you for another round of pitching when the chips seem to be down. What they won't or can't do is guarantee you the results you desire.

Researching and contracting with a publicist is, at its most fundamental level, no different than choosing health insurance or negotiating to buy a home. The ancient Romans had a saying that still exists today. In Latin, it's *caveat emptor,* or as many of us know, "let the buyer beware!"

A good publicist should also interview you. Longtime publicist and media strategist Stan Rosenfield, who represents the likes of Robert De Niro, George Clooney, Andy Garcia, and Patricia Clarkson, says that he takes on clients who have similar sensitivities to his area of PR expertise. "I wouldn't take on a rock act and a rock act wouldn't come to us. We wouldn't do a very good job because that isn't our area of expertise."

When Publicists Miss the Mark

Hey, that title sounds like a Fox TV show, along the lines of *When Animals Attack,* doesn't it? Maybe I should pitch it? Hmmm. All right, all right, even a seasoned producer and professional media consultant is allowed to have a bum idea or two. But I made this joke to illustrate a point: everybody, in every walk of life, fails on occasion. Hiring even an experienced PR agent is no guarantee to ward off snafus and disasters, as we shall see.

It's common sense time again: there are almost fifty thousand PR and publicity agents in the U.S. Some of them will be stars, others will be highly effective at their craft, many will be perfectly competent and trustworthy, but some may not be any good at all. I cannot tell you how many times I have had a publicist pitch a client to me when that client's hooks are totally mismatched to my show. Like the ugly stepsisters in the Cinderella story, no amount of persuasion or pushing will get a great big foot into a petite glass slipper! Now, while individuals who pitch their own material often make such targeting mistakes, I recognize that everybody has a learning curve and cut them some slack. But publicists who pitch without bothering to find out what a show's style and format are really get my goat. They are not only doing me (or any producer) a professional discourtesy, they are doing their own clients an irreparable disservice.

PR firms can also mess up in other ways. Once upon a time, a publicity firm decided that its clients simply must be with-it and up-to-the-moment, not to mention technologically hip. So they sent out a valued client's demo reel (the client had something to sell) in the "business card mini-CD" format. "Who needs stuffy old VHS tape demo reels?" they might have proclaimed, "We're totally cutting edge here!"

The brand-spanking-new reels were sent out across this fair land of ours. And in production offices across the land (offices that could have booked the publicist's client and helped sell whatever doodad they were selling) producers and assistants and interns all oohed and aahed over the cute little mini-CDs. But love is fickle, and as soon as the producers discovered that the mini-CDs would not play on their computers, let alone insert into the Macs, the with-it, up-to-the-moment gadgets went straight into the trash can. Nobody ever found out what it was that the publicity firm's client was selling.

Harsh, but true. The reel in question did indeed get canned. That particular show I was working on at the time was in heavy deadline mode: shows to tape, guests to book, and looming disasters to snatch from the teeth of ruination. Who has time to fiddle about with a fancy new technology that didn't even insert into a Mac? Of course, we might have tried contacting the firm, but we were all so frantically overloaded with work we forgot. And the *caveat emptor* punch line here? The firm never even bothered to contact us to ask what our reaction to their client was. Talk about slacking off...

Furthermore, many publicists like to send material in electronic format (email) because it is cost-effective. But there's a conscious action, in my opinion, that takes place when a producer has to stop and open a priority envelope as opposed to sorting through fifty-plus emails. At least when a producer receives a package, we feel singled out, whereas an email is one mouse-click away from the delete file.

How Do I Find a Publicist?

If you live in a small town, go to your local library and check out phone books from a larger city near you. Those of you who are wired for Internet access can perform this basic function at home, but bear in mind that some individual PR agents or smaller agencies may not have Web presence, or you may have to wade through scores of search engine results to get to what you need.

Of course, you may live in the wilds of Alaska, so you may worry that publicists are scarce in your neck of the woods. The Internet then becomes a vital tool for research. But think about this: a great many organizations, charities, politicians, unions, companies, and corporations employ public relations staff. Any PR professional, even when not experienced with trolling the media outlets you are targeting, will have contacts who may be able to help you, whether by taking you on as a client, or by pointing you at a colleague or firm that they recommend. So no matter how far from the center of the universe you may live, if you have a phone and library access, you can get in on the publicity game.

> For more information about public relations, go to www.prsa.org, the website of the Public Relations Society of American (PRSA). The society has over twenty thousand members organized into over one hundred chapters representing individuals, businesses, government, nonprofit agencies, and many more entities.

Can I Be My Own Publicist?

Can you be your own publicist? Are you kidding me? *There isn't anything we've been talking about here that you couldn't do yourself, especially when it comes to allocating time and money and resources.* Of course you can act as your own publicist, but think like a producer!

Seriously folks, *Get on TV* is designed as a do-it-yourself guide to becoming a TV guest or expert. And I have booked scads, heaps, bunches and...well, scores of guests who had no publicity agent. As we have seen, all it really takes beyond something worthwhile to pitch is organization, preparation, confidence and persistence. Most of you, if my seminars are any indication, are highly motivated self-starters with a can-do attitude and an entrepreneurial spirit. Simply by picking up this book and buying it, you are already beginning your journey to get on TV.

Even if you can easily afford a publicist, and you find one to take you on, I'd still recommend at least *considering* starting out under your own steam and carrying this knowledge with you, as it will protect your investment.

PERSONAL STORY: INTERVIEW WITH ANAT BARON

Anat Baron appeared on national TV, radio, and magazines as "The Travel Fanatic" in 2000–01 before 9/11 changed the travel industry forever. She's an executive producer at Ducks in a Row Entertainment Corporation in Beverly Hills, CA. She says that she never had much luck with publicists.

"Like anything in life, it's all about expectations. If you're looking to get clips as a measure of success, you may be satisfied. For me, because of the circumstances at the time I wanted big hits—national papers, magazines, and TV shows. I came in with lists, articles, show topics. I was totally prepared. And I was very clear that I had big expectations. Despite my warning of, 'Please don't take me on unless you think you can deliver—quickly,' only one firm turned me down."

In Anat's experience, she believes that potential TV guests should know if they've ever represented anyone like you and how many clients they have and how many people service them. You should know whom they have access to and their reputation in the media. You should also be permitted to talk to past and present clients.

Most important, you should know and understand what they'll do for you—who will work on your account, how often you'll hear from them, if they have a Plan A and a Plan B for you. So that you are clear about the expectations.

Anat decided to handle her own publicity because she felt that no one could sell her better than she could. We all probably know somebody who is so self-confident, so sure of themselves, that they could sell a truckload of snow to a Siberian. Watching people with a seemingly innate ability to communicate and work the room can be humbling for those of us who are less extroverted. But not being extroverted does not mean that you are an introvert either. You may be great in interview situations, yet perform poorly at the cold-calling that gets you in the door for the interview in the first place. Which brings me to an interesting point…if selling yourself is not your strong suit, but you are confident you could still deliver on television (obviously the most important thing at the end of the day), then a publicist might be your best solution.

Final Thoughts on Publicists

Writing about the role of a publicist is tricky. As a TV producer, I have many strong, necessary, and vital relationships with publicists that have carried me throughout my history on many television shows. The show that I currently oversee is interdependent on relationships with celebrity publicists with high-profile A-list guests. So don't misunderstand my words of caution. Publicists rock, they really do. Just don't feel that if you can't afford one, or if you can't get one to represent you, that you're climbing from the bottom rung of the ladder.

You too, can act as your own publicist! Now get out there and work those phones, faxes, and word processors: there are guest and expert slots to be booked each and every day.

The Fine Line Between Persistence and Stalking

They're sitting in my production office. Right over there: the two Federal Express boxes in the corner. They cost you twenty-three dollars in postage fees *each*. And yes, you have every right to know if my staff has looked at your material. You've tried phone calls, but we're taping five shows this week and next, so we have been unable to return your call. What do you do next?

Send us a postcard, a small little note, just a polite reminder that you are awaiting a response of some kind. Remember our branding lessons: it'd be best if your brand identification matched all the way through. So a postcard bought at a bookstore or a supermarket is a fair enough reminder, but a custom-printed card with your headshot, logo, or other signifying visual information would be the best possible approach. The card must be "accessorized" to whatever is in the FedEx boxes. This creative approach not only makes it easy for us to instantly identify you, but it also reinforces your message, story, product, etc. If my staff has in fact already opened your FedEx packages, a brand-matched postcard will jump-start their recollection—"Oh, I remember this press kit." An eye-catching card may also possibly give your submission a second wind. Sometimes decent pitches fall through the cracks due to sheer busyness on our part.

So you send a postcard as a small follow-up. Now, in a weird way, you still are affecting a relationship. It's not a positive one yet, but it's still a relationship. You're still in the door and this is okay, this is protocol. It is not considered pushy behavior; you are not stalking. Not yet, anyway.

I know that you badly want to get booked on my show or any show that you have your heart set on, but bear in mind that politeness and grace are always much appreciated. There is only a hop, a skip, and maybe a jump from perseverance to pushiness. And I should know, because I was once the inadvertent stalker of a poor, freaked-out network executive. I will share my moment of blistering shame with you in the hopes that you can avoid falling into the pit of everlasting, ever-squirming social embarrassment.

Well, I once stalked somebody. I don't know how it happened, or what came over me, but I do know that I've never done it since! The scene is a seminar that I was attending (this was before I began to organize my own media seminars). One of the featured attendees was a network executive that I wanted to pitch a project to. A third party introduced me to this woman after the seminar meeting was concluded. We continued talking as we left the hotel and headed out into the parking garage. Here is where that fine line lies. We were chatting amiably, right? Networking is one of the purposes of such seminars, so it's not as if I cornered this person in a restaurant and pitched to her. But as we entered the parking structure's entrance, a small voice piped up in the back of my mind—"I know I should not be here." It was just a boundary that I knew I should not cross. I should have said thank you and good-bye and "I'll be in touch." But I didn't. Her car turned out to be right there by the entrance. I had inadvertently followed this woman to her car. *I had become a stalker!*

I tell you this anecdote in jest. The woman was gracious and relaxed, and did not seem bothered that our inside conversation had moved outside. But I had breached my own protocols as to good manners. And maybe she was exceptionally polite herself, and was hiding her disapproval. The project I had pitched never did go anywhere with her network, but that's just one of those things.

The irony of this situation is that a day or two later I was having a conversation with another producer who was saying, "I hate doing those seminars. You always get stalked because someone always follows you to your car." And I probably smiled a little guiltily and agreed!

The point of this story is that there is a line in such situations, and you don't want to cross it. Bombarding my staff with phone calls and messages concerning your aforementioned FedEx submissions is the long-distance equivalent of following us into a parking lot to our cars.

In terms of sending flowers or gifts, I think it's a great idea. As producers, we are not supposed to take payola, although I have yet to see a producer turn a gift down. Such gifts are actually a good idea if they directly relate to a product you are pitching, especially if your product is gimmicky and fun.

I was once sent a box of rock crystal deodorant. I was not going to put this product on TV as it did not quite match my show's format at that particular time, so the crystal deodorant sat in my office for months and months. But I passed it out to everybody, and it became a running joke in the office. "Here, you smell? Take some rock crystal deodorant." People actually tried it and *liked it.* The product wound up in other show's offices and to this day I still have producers tell me that they switched to rock crystal deodorants. So while I did not book the purveyor of the crystals for my show, the product was much talked about and eventually was put on the air as a product giveaway to the audience during a humorous segment. So just because you do not hear from a show does not necessarily mean that you have not made an impact.

When all is said and done, a simple postcard reminder will indeed suffice. Those of you operating on a shoestring budget can breathe a sigh of relief. As far as phone call follow-ups go, use your best social instincts to judge when you may be about to cross from being persistent to being annoying. We will do our very best to get back to you, but sometimes (in fact many, many times) there is not enough time in the day to do so for every potential guest who calls. If you haven't heard from a producer or staff member for X weeks/months, and have made four attempts to follow up with no success, then it's a good bet that your pitch is not right for our show. No news, in this scenario, is not good news. But if you find yourself feeling annoyed or angry over a nonresponse, remain polite, because you never know who is going to keep you in mind for another show, or who may have passed your press kit along to a colleague.

As always, be persistent and keep plugging away: that perfect match between format, hook, and timing may be just around the corner.

Creating Professional Relationships of Lasting Value

Ultimately, your television career pathway is not a finite "trophy hunt" in which you seek to collect an appearance on this show or that one. You should see your career more organically, as something that grows and flourishes over the years and through many different seasons. So your investment of time is not about each show, it's about the relationships with the producers that you create.

In my corner of the television industry, we're a close-knit group of people who know each other really well. We also know each other's careers, and frequently help one another out with suggestions and tips about guests. We'll do lunch or hang out at an industry function and throw a guest or expert's name out on a table. Nine times out of ten, we've all produced that person at some point. We'll inevitably chat about how a guest or expert is: easygoing and fun to work with, or difficult and high maintenance. That's right, we gossip about you! That's why it is important to behave politely at all times when booked on a show. A negative impression might follow you to your next potential booking, and be a deciding factor in being rejected. It happens, believe me.

So you may fail to get on a series of your targeted shows, but if you have laid the solid groundwork outlined in this book, and your pitch is interesting, rest assured we may well wind up talking about you outside of the realm of the shows on which we work. You may be the next hot tip I receive from a colleague, or I may pass your details along to another show across town (or across the country).

When you get right down to it, your television career path is not about shows, it is about creating lasting relationships with producers. Establish a professional bond and you'll follow a producer around from show to show. Today's associate producer in a local radio show might be working on the next *Oprah* or *Dr. Phil* a few years on down the line.

STRATEGY TIP

By participating in our production process via thoughtful submissions, ideas, and potential hooks, you are creating a relationship with our show and our producing staff *even if we are not responding to you.*

If you have what it takes to be on TV and participate in our production process in good faith, we will wind up talking about you amongst ourselves. This discussion may or may not lead to a booking, but we might recommend you to another show that's looking for guests like you.

Remember this: we never forget a quality potential guest even if we fail to book that person season after season. Politeness, process, and persistence will pay off eventually.

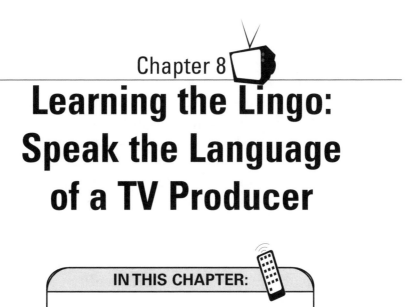

Chapter 8

Learning the Lingo: Speak the Language of a TV Producer

IN THIS CHAPTER:

○ The A to Z of TV

Now that you've learned how to put your pitch into practice, this chapter shares with you the behind-the-scenes language of a very *interesting* industry that you are about to become a part of...

There's an old saying that goes "When in Rome, do as the Romans do." In order to understand a person's culture, you must understand their language, which will allow you to understand the way that they think. It is a dead giveaway during a pitch when the common language isn't mutually understood. As the guest or expert, you must position yourself as an insider, no matter if you are a novice. Otherwise, you will come across as an outsider trying to get in. Think of this chapter as a handy phrase book that translates "televisionese" into English. The following list of definitions might look intimidating—like flashbacks to grammar school vocabulary exams—but I assure you that as you read on, you will gain a deep insight into this ironic, sometimes humorous, often insularly industry, and you'll come out understanding their nature with a greater respect, a keen eye, and ready for your performance.

The A to Z of TV

AFTRA: The American Federation of Television and Radio Artists (AFTRA) is a national labor union representing nearly 80,000 performers, journalists, and other artists working in the entertainment and news media. AFTRA's scope of representation covers broadcast, public and cable television (news, sports and weather, drama and comedy, soaps, talk and variety shows, documentaries, children's programming, reality and game shows); radio (news, commercials, hosted programs); sound recordings (CDs, singles, Broadway cast albums, audiobooks); "non-broadcast" and industrial material as well as Internet and digital programming. Why is this an important term? Because you, my friends, may one day be a member of AFTRA as you move from beginner to professional guest or expert. So, when appropriate, I'd like to say—"Welcome to the club!" I look forward to giving you the double top-secret AFTRA handshake.

Agent: One who is authorized to act for or in the place of another as a business representative. Do you need an agent? That depends. If your goal is to have your own TV show, then eventually, you will need an agent to help handle your career and hook you up with the right networks. *An agent is not at all required to become a TV guest or expert.*

Anyone have "eyes on…?": Walkie-talkie lingo for "Has anyone seen…?" Hopefully, you'll be where we expect you to be, so nobody will be asking after your whereabouts.

Assemble/Assembly: After a show is taped, it enters the postproduction phase, during which an editor puts all the visual, graphical, and sound elements together to make a finished show. Shows are often not taped in the order that they are scripted to be in, so assembly happens when all the footage is placed in the correct scripted sequence. So an assembly is the rough rock from which an editor sculpts the final smooth and finished product.

Associate Director (AD): Think of the producing staff as a show's designers and planners. This makes the show's director the on-the-scene ringleader of our circus. And an associate director is the ringleader's right-hand man (or woman). They carry out the director's instructions, cue video, time the show, and are generally indispensable, not to mention very, very busy during a shoot.

Audition: Well, we all know what an audition is, right? You strut your stuff or pitch your story, product, hook, etc., and we listen and/or watch, then evaluate what's on offer. The word comes from the Latin term *audire* meaning "to hear." Your press kit materials and show reel are a form of audition, as is a pre-interview. Remember: always be prepared and put your best foot forward.

Avid: Avid is a widely utilized editing system that enables producers to assemble the raw footage from a show, then whittle it down to the target length. When it was introduced in the late 1980s, the technology was revolutionary because it was *non-linear.* This means that any shot can be moved about, duplicated, cut out, and put back in all with the click of a mouse. Once upon a time, editing a show together was a *linear* process, like putting together train tracks. If you wanted to change a shot, a lengthy process was involved. The Avid Company offers editing software for PC and Mac home computer editing systems, which means that you can use their products to assemble and revise your show reel. Their website address is: www.avid.com

Barista: Someone who is professionally trained in the art of espresso preparation. Television production staffers eat, sleep, and breathe caffeinated beverages in order to maintain long hours. If you overhear us in raptures over a double nonfat soymilk chai latte as prepared by our favorite barista, you will know whereof we speak.

The Bay: The editing booth, where editors roam. This is where a taped show gets its finishing touches, a complex process known as postproduction.

Betacam: Hmmm. I think I'll hold off providing you with a thorough explanation of the evolution of videotape systems! Suffice to say that

Betacam is a type of camera often used in a show's production: it utilizes a specific type of video tape which, once upon a time, was a rival to the ubiquitous VHS system. Beta tapes offer higher image quality than VHS, which is why they're used on the production of television shows. Eventually, all TV shows and movies will be shot *digitally* and the tape systems will go the way of the dodo and the dinosaur.

Bid: A price offer for a service. When the hiring cycle begins, a show's production coordinator or line producer will take bids from prospective crew members. Or they might compare bids from companies offering satellite services, such as fully equipped, remote broadcast trucks, etc.

Bio: A bio, or biography, is part of your press kit. We can skip your childhood, high school, and young adult adventures in favor of a brief— no, make that very brief—summary of who you are and why you are pitching to me. Include personal details only if they are directly relevant, as was the case with lawyer Michelle Lee Flores (see her sample bio in chapter 5), whose early courtroom trauma motivated her career choice. The most important part of a bio is to capture your essence. An overview of what you have done on your field of endeavor is important, but not as important as getting your flavor to jump off a piece of paper.

The Bird: A slang term for a communications satellite. The Bird allows a signal to be instantaneously bounced from one side of the planet to the other. This is how a host at a taping in LA can talk to an actor on location in England.

Blue Cards: A show's host holds blue index cards that help him or her keep track of information, such as a guest's name, or any bullet points (main topical points) relevant to a segment. David Letterman is famous for frisbee-ing his blue cards through the window behind his desk. Why are the cards blue? It's a technical issue; white cards throw off the video camera's ability to balance out color brightness scales. To a camera, which has various automatic functions, a white card looks like a brilliant flash of pure light, and it will try and compensate for this by closing the camera aperture and making everything look "dark" and overcast. Fortunately, gleaming capped teeth do not seem to bother the cameras at all!

Booked, Booking: A booking is a scheduled appearance or performance. All bookings are subject to unexpected change or even cancellation. In fact, cancelled bookings are common, so prepare yourself. You will get cancelled at many points in your media career (see chapter 9).

Boom: What happens when you fall down! Sorry, I couldn't resist that one. A *boom* is a type of microphone (*boom mike*) that is attached to a long "pole." It enables the *boom man* to position the microphone anywhere in the studio. So when an audience member asks a question, a boom mike is often hanging above their heads, just out of view of the camera. Boom mikes are famous for bomping unsuspecting folks in the forehead. But as they are usually contained within foam coverings, this doesn't really hurt much. Booms are primarily in the field, not as often in a studio.

The Booth: Our nickname for the control room, where the director watches all the camera point-of-view feeds at once, and decides which shots to use for the line cut, a rough assembly of footage from the taping.

Breakdown: A) A list of items, such as equipment that is rented for a location shoot or the content items for that day's show taping. B) A sad occurrence for those of us who may be sentimental. When a show has completed its run or gets cancelled, the crew breaks down the set to make way for whatever new use the studio space will be put to next.

Breaking News: A news event that is occurring as it is reported in radio or TV. Sometimes a news broadcast will cut short whatever they are presenting to deal with breaking news. Non-news programming is sometimes pre-empted by breaking news. Worst case scenario: you've just been presented on the TV show of your dreams but breaking news about a runaway moose knocks the program off the air!

Budget: The amount of money allocated for a particular show or segment. Due to the high cost of producing a television show that employs up to one hundred people, funds are very tight, so don't eat too many of those complimentary peanuts in the green room!

Bumpers: This is *not* a term. I once had a slightly bossy, know-it-all guest refer to bump-ins (see the next entry) as bumpers. It's not a big deal, but given her general tone, it just bugged me. So the lesson here is this: be familiar with a producer's language lexicon, but don't pepper your conversation with terminology. It is worse to get it wrong than to not use it at all.

Bump-In/Bump-Out: Bump-ins and bump-outs are the descendants of "Stay tuned, we'll be right back after this message" announcements. They set up or lead out from a segment, and usually reveal what's coming up next, a factoid relevant to the segment, or sometimes video montages (an edited series of images) of moments we've already seen on the show, which are recaps for viewers who have tuned in late. Bumps range from ten seconds to thirty seconds.

Callback: A follow-up phone call or meeting in regards to a booking, pre-interview, or audition, as in "I'll give you a callback early next week and we'll go over your details again."

Call Sheet: A show's map and bible, without which all would collapse into chaos. A call sheet tells everybody from staff to guests what time they have to arrive in the studio. It also lists everybody's contact information and cell phone numbers.

Call Time: The specific time we have scheduled for you to arrive in the studio, after which you will prep for the show.

Cameraman: A person who operates one of the many television cameras in the studio. On talk shows, the cameramen know where to point their cameras because everything has been scripted and planned in advance with an open mind for spontaneity. On live TV shows, cameramen receive instructions via radio earphones. They will always try to get your best side!

Casting Director: A person who supervises the casting of films, dramatic productions, plays, commercials, and reality TV shows.

Clean Tape: A videotape that is blank and has never been used (and erased). Using and erasing a tape multiple times begins to degrade the tape's ability to hold a clear image. When updating your reels, it's a safe bet to always use fresh, clean tapes.

Clearance: Authorization to use a specific item, such as a clip from a movie or TV show, or a musical recording. For example, if we are planning to show one of your family photos, we have to have signed legal clearance from everybody in the picture in order to air it. Clearing such items protects a show from lawsuits.

Clips: 1) A segment of a larger show or series of images. *America's Funniest Home Videos* plays home short video clips of amusing activity. The legal rights to use these clips must be cleared for use on television. 2) You will place pre-edited clips of your TV appearances on your show reel. As time goes on, new clips will be added, and old clips will be retired.

Coordinator: Usually the production coordinator, who handles the logistical operations when a show tapes: which guest is arriving when, when to feed the crew, and where to put that pesky elephant until its segment is ready to roll.

Craft Services: Aka catering service. This is where the food is, usually available only to the crew and staff. These services utilize mobile catering trucks that can be set up in studio parking lots.

Cranes: A device onto which cameras are mounted in order to provide them with greater range of motion. When you see a shot speeding above the heads of a studio audience and towards the host onstage, this is a crane shot, aka a jib shot.

Crew: A show's crew is all the professionals involved in the actual studio taping shoot. They range from directors and cameramen to sound engineers and makeup artists. The host and producing staff are not part of the crew, although we all work closely together.

Cue Card: Large cards that the talent (aka the hosts) reads from during a taping, enabling them to perform scripted introductions without having to memorize lines. Marlon Brando utilized cue cards during the production of the motion picture *The Godfather.* But this wasn't because he was unprepared; it was all part of his method acting technique. Brando didn't want to commit his lines to memory so that they wouldn't seem stale when he spoke them.

Cut/Cutting: This is a common editing term indicating a visual shift between two different camera viewpoints. "Cutting" a show together is another way of saying that it is being assembled or edited together.

Deliverables: The master tape (see listing) that is delivered to a studio or network so that a program can be distributed and aired locally or nationally.

Development: A period in a show's evolution prior to production. A show is "in development" when network executives of star hosts are figuring out format and content issues.

DGA: The Directors Guild of America, a national union of film, television, and commercial directors. Many studios cannot legally hire a director who is not a member of the union. The DGA negotiates with the studios on behalf of its members.

Digi Beta: A system that records digitally on Betacam cassettes, as opposed to old school *analog* recording methods. Don't worry about the technical side! Digi Beta is cutting edge and the picture quality is as good as it gets.

Digital/Digitized: The root word here is *digits,* i.e., numbers. In a digital sound recording (like a CD), sound waves are translated into numbers, which makes for much better fidelity that other *analog* forms of recording (LP albums). Image digitization is much the same. Digital pictures are crisper and cleaner than images shot on film or video. *Digitized* is the process whereby an analog source (and LP, or a super-8 movie, or a VHS recording) is translated to digital format. Recently, movies such as *The Incredibles* and the final *Star Wars* prequel were projected with digital technology in selected cinemas. One day, film projectors will be the stuff or art houses and cinematheques, and every cineplex will show only digitally projected movies. Nowadays, most good camcorders record digitally.

Director: In the television field (fictional dramas and comedies aside) directors are key organizers of the shoot. They block each show with the producing staff and the camera crew, and ensure that the show's visual identity is maintained.

Director of Photography (DP): A movie's "photographer," who lights every scene. This job requires technical proficiency as well as an artistic component. A DP's job has been likened to "painting with light." TV shows such as *CSI* and *Malcolm in the Middle* use DPs, but news programs and chat shows have lighting directors (see that listing for more info).

Down a few generations: Just as photocopying a photocopy, then photocopying that copy reduces the clarity of image quality, a dub (tape copy) of a dub (tape copy) instead of a dub from a master tape will not look as hot as the original. A copy of a copy might be fine, but if further copies (dubs) are made in turn, subsequent generations of tapes will look fuzzy and unprofessional. Always make a copy of your show reel from the master tape, and not from a copy, no matter how inconvenient or expensive this may be.

Dub/Dubs: Now this is a multi-purpose word! In my neck of the woods, *to dub* is to make a copy of a VHS, Beta, or digital tape. After you appear on my show, I will send you a dub copy that you can use in your show reel. Here are two more primary meanings for the term, all of which are slightly related. 1. To add music, sound effects, or rerecorded dialogue to a film, radio, or television production. 2. To provide a motion picture or television program with a new soundtrack featuring dialogue in a different language (some foreign movies are released with subtitled, whole others are *dubbed* into English).

Edit Bay: A room that will most likely be stacked to the rafters with expensive machines used in the editing process, as well as less expensive things like snacks and couches to nap on. This is where editors assemble a show (or movie, or commercial, or music video) using systems like Avid. Producers can pop in unexpectedly (or by arrangement!) to see how everything is turning out.

Editor: After the production phase, during which a show is taped (aka the shoot), it enters the postproduction phase. Editors assemble the show, decide which camera angles are best for any given moment of screen time, cut out all the parts when the camera filmed nothing special, add in any music that is needed, and put in graphics (the show's titles, credits, segment titles, guest's names, etc.). Editors tend to work very long shifts and have been known to edit through the night to meet a deadline. They may be paler than other key crewmembers, and also tend to be quieter than, say cameramen or gaffers, who tend to be fond of "big fish" tall tales.

Elements: A general term for any and all components of a show aside from the content (guests; topics, etc.). Elements are props, music, and graphics.

Emmy: An award given by the Academy of Television Arts and Sciences to the best shows and performers from a given year. I've been nominated twice. Maybe the third time will be the charm!

ENG: Electronic news gathering is simply a fancy way of describing what happens when a crew is sent out to cover a news story. This differs from more traditional forms of print newsgathering, such as phone interviews and research.

EPK: An electronic press kit is a video sales tape that publicists send out for their clients. EPKs contain clips that cover their client's career, story, or specialty. These clips are given pre-clearance to be used on any television program, from talk to news formats.

Evergreen: A taped segment that is always "fresh" at any time of the year. In other words, they do not deal with seasonal or cyclical subjects.

Executive Producer: The most senior executive on a show or movie. EPs oversee projects and usually act as the liaison between a show or movie's production staff and a studio or network. You do not want to pitch an EP, unless they invite you to or you encounter them in a seminar setting. Aim lower on the production chain.

Final Cut Pro: This is an amazing Mac application that enables you to edit at home with an array of tools that approaches those available to professionals. All you need is a camcorder, a Mac, and Final Cut Pro and you can make a very flashy show reel (or music video, or movie) complete with graphics and mixed sound.

Final Draft: In relation to a script, this would be the last version minted prior to a show's taping. Also known as a shooting draft. Final Draft is also the name of a software word processing application enables the user to write correctly formatted scripts for film and television. Available for PC and Mac.

Fix it in Post: An oft-heard refrain on a shoot, meaning, *"we don't have the time or money to re-shoot this part where the host falls off the stage or the guest is seized by a sudden fit of giggling, so we'll fix it in post."* In other words, we'll be editing out (removing) that part in postproduction. *"Fix it in post"* applies to a wide array of mostly minor problems, and occasionally major ones. The phrase only applies to taped shows. On live TV, what you see is what you get.

Floor: The camera zone on the periphery of the stage set. This area needs to be clear at all times for moving cameras, roaming hosts, or audience response shots and for producers who produce the segment from this space.

Gaffer: A lighting electrician on a motion picture or television set. Works under the lighting director. Also rigs the studio's lighting system.

Getting Picked Up: No, this has nothing to do with singles bars, thank you very much. *Getting picked up* is what happens when a television pilot show (a sample TV show) gets an order to go into production, or when a show that's on hiatus gets renewed for another production cycle.

Graphics: Pictures or printed words that are superimposed on a television picture. A show's logo and credits are graphics. Network and cable newscasts tend to make heavy use of sophisticated graphics, which include animation. Graphics capability is available with some home editing systems. Do your homework before you buy!

Green: An inexperienced or naïve guest.

Green Room: Guest dressing room.

Grip: A crew member who lays down camera tracks, or builds camera platforms in a motion picture or television production. Sometimes, grips actually push a camera in what is called a dolly shot or a tracking shot.

Hard Out: A *hard out* is the time when a taping absolutely *must* conclude. For instance, a *hard* out might be due to the host's commitment to be elsewhere, or to catch an important (and very occasionally, not so important!) flight. If a show's taping begins to edge too close to a *hard out* time, a segment may be shortened or dropped entirely. As is the case with any cancellation, do not take this personally!

HDTV: High-definition television. In layman's terms, this is a television format that has twice as much detail and picture quality as current formats and models. An HDTV is shaped like a rectangular movie screen rather than an "old fashioned" square TV set. Some programs are broadcast in HDTV format, but trust me kiddos, *this is the wave of the future.* Everybody and their grandmother knows what a DVD is nowadays, but ten years ago, when the format was commercially available, nobody had heard of it outside of technology geeks and movie connoisseurs. Within the foreseeable future, HDTV will be as ubiquitous as DVDs are in the present day.

Headshot: A photograph featuring just face and/or head and shoulders; part of your press kit. I suggest using a professional photographer for your headshot, and no, I don't mean K-Mart! Look in the Yellow Pages for shutterbugs that specialize in headshots.

Hi8: The best possible analog camcorder recording tapes available to the public. If you are in the market for a new camcorder, *go digital.* Analog recording will soon be a quaint and fondly remembered twentieth-century relic, like a 45-rpm single records, mood rings, and lava lamps!

Home Base: This is the name for the area of the set in the studio where the host and guests sit together. This is where it all happens: we've worked hard to set everything up for the taping and you've worked hard to get here.

Honey Wagons: Also known as star trailers, both terms being brand names for mobile trailers that have multiple functions, such as dressing rooms, or green rooms (see entry). This is where key talent can relax in air-conditioned peace. But you don't have to be a star to work in one. Costume and makeup use the trailers when on location, i.e., filming or taping outside a studio environment. And no, you will not get a star trailer as a perk until you can go toe-to-toe with Dr. Phil.

Hosts: A television or radio "emcee," aka MC, aka "Master of Ceremonies." Hosts are the face of a television program, and a show's format is usually tailored to the host's persona and interests. Hosts are not usually directly involved in developing individual show segments, so pitching to them is not a practical approach. As is the case with an executive producer (see chapter 2), your best bet is to target the production staff that work for these two key figures.

IA: A shortened form of IATSE, which is itself a shortened version of (take a deep breath) The International Alliance of Theatrical Stage Employees, Moving Picture Technicians, Artists and Allied Crafts of the United States, Its Territories and Canada. This powerful and celebrated union has been in existence since 1893.

IFB: This stands for *Interruptible Feedback.* This is a tiny radio receiver that a host (or news anchor) wears in their ear, via which a show's producer or director can broadcast information or instructions. It was well known that when Ricki Lake began her long and distinguished career as a host, her producers fed her questions to ask her guests via an IFB. Once she mastered her craft, she relied much less on the handy "crib sheet" device.

Interstitial: A short segment, usually about a minute long, that plays within a larger program's airtime. For example, CNN runs *Money Minute* interstitials throughout many of its shows, usually before or after a commercial break.

Intro: How a host will verbally introduce you in any given segment. You have a right to know what information a host will be using, and how this info will be presented.

ISO: Stands for Isolated Camera. An ISO is a camera that is exclusively focused on a specific guest or the host. While the show's other cameras track in and out and pan (pivot) from guest to guest (like watching the back and forth of a tennis game), an ISO camera targets one person without interruption. This is "insurance" for the postproduction editing process, for a moving camera can miss an important reaction or comment from a guest or host, whereas an ISO won't miss a trick.

Jibs: Part of a camera crane or boom microphone platform. If you are very tall, you may be instructed to watch out for jib arms, but this is rather unlikely. *Dancing a jib* is what happens when one is knocked senseless by a collision with a jib and begins to dance uncontrollably. This potentially embarrassing escapade can be "fixed in post." (Just kidding!)

Lav: Abbreviation for lavaliere microphone: a small mike hung around the neck of the user, or affixed like a broach or tiepin. Eliminates the need for a boom mike looming above one's head.

Lighting Director: A lighting director is responsible for lighting the studio set and the audience. This is vastly more complicated that it may sound. For instance, they use scores of lights at different angles, but must ensure that there are absolutely no areas of shadow on set. The DP has his or her own crew of gaffers, who move and set the lighting equipment, and best boys, who handle the complex electrical connections and needs of the studio's lighting system. The camera crew also works under a LD's "command," but it is the show's director that calls all the visual shots.

Lighting Pack: A technical term for the array of lighting equipment rented for a show or motion picture. The lighting pack for an exterior shoot or taping will differ from one for an interior shoot.

Line Cut: A rough edit made during a show's taping that is a compilation of ISO (see entry) shots. The director "calls" what camera points of view to use as the show tapes and the technical director executes this sequence. The Line Cut tape is used during the postproduction-editing phase where fixes and tweaks are made.

Line Producer: A member of a producing staff who oversees all of the non-creative aspects of a production such as crew, technology rentals, and scheduling. These producers have nothing to do with booking guests, so you do not pitch to a LP if you corner them at a party or on a bus. They will only refer you to the appropriate member of the production team (if you are polite and smell nice).

Live: A live production is one that simultaneously tapes, broadcasts, and is received by your TV (or radio). Any mistakes on a live broadcast are visible to the viewing audience. One of the most shocking moments on live television occurred in 1963, when Jack Ruby shot and killed JFK's assassin Lee Harvey Oswald in the basement of a Dallas police station. On the other hand, the 1969 moon landing was a live event that was a defining moment in humanity's history that was shared by everybody watching television.

Live-to-Tape: Some shows like to have the ambience of a live broadcast. *Saturday Night Live* is a live broadcast, but *The Tonight Show* is taped before a live audience for broadcast several hours later. Live-to-tape shows can easily be edited to fix mistakes or instances of profanity, for example. A host like Leno or Letterman will behave as if a segment had a limited amount of time prior to commercial break, but this is in fact a fiction. If a segment runs long, it can be edited down to the proper length. Daytime talk shows like *Oprah* or *Ellen* are also live-to-tape.

Loaded: When the tapes are loaded into the cameras and ready to roll, we say they are *loaded.*

Location Fee: For a shoot or taping in a public place, a location fee will go to a city, county, or state government. In private locations, the fee is paid to whoever owns the premises.

Location Scout: A person employed to seek out specific locations as requested by a TV show or motion picture production. Location scouts scour cities and suburbs armed with a digital camera, so they can take multiple pictures of a cool 1950s diner or a picturesque barn or whatnot. Current technology makes it possible to transmit these photos directly to a production office.

Location Shoot: A shoot or taping that does not take place within the confines of a studio lot. Location shoots are expensive, as they require permits, extra security, traffic cops, specialized lighting packages, and various talent and crew trailers and vehicles such as generator trucks. A location shoot has a circus-like atmosphere: they can be as fun as they are crazy-hectic.

Lock Picture: The point after which no changes can be made to an edited program, although sound and music can be added or fiddled with.

Look Live: Aha! I'm going to reveal a television secret to you now. Look live is a cheat technique whereby a show uses a pretaped shot to simulate a live satellite-relayed shot. This is done when an actual satellite-relayed shot is too expensive to procure (which is a lot of the time). So when you watch a show and the host checks in with a reporter or staff member in another state, you may be watching some television trickery.

Lower Thirds: Lower thirds, also known as chyrons, are text graphics located in the bottom third of a TV screen. They usually present a guest's name and specialty or POV (Bob Smith, Sports Fitness Expert). Upper Thirds are used less frequently to indicate information such as "Courtesy of Corporation X or Network Y." *Chyron* is actually a brand name. The Chyron Corporation developed on-air graphics in 1970 and they are the industry leader throughout the world.

Manager: A manager is like an agent, but they are not legally authorized to actually cut a contracted deal for you. There is a fine line between agents and managers these days, and the two fields are often in opposition as to who has the right to do what. An agent is best qualified to try and sell your work (book, product) or promote your career. Agents also advise their clients as to shaping a career path or business plan, but this is where managers come into play. A manager may have much more experience molding a career than an agent has, especially a junior agent. So think of a manager as a person who advises you what kind of house to buy and in what area, while an agent actually handles the nuts and bolts of the sale. Anybody can declare himself or herself to be a manager, but agents have to earn a regulated license to practice their profession.

Marketing: Literally, taking your goods to a marketplace. In terms of media, the marketplace is radio, television, or motion pictures. Your goods are yourself as a media personality or expert, or the story you have to tell, or a product you have to sell. It's a sophisticated field of endeavor, but that does not mean that you can't take a do-it-yourself approach to marketing yourself to any number or media outlets.

Master: A master is the complete and final dub of a show that is ready for broadcast. How does a master tape of a show get distributed across the country to hundreds of network and affiliate stations? The tapes are digitally broadcast, and each station receives this signal transmission and records a high quality copy or dub of the source master tape.

Mixer: A mixer is a device that mixes together sounds and music, and balances out all the varying levels of loudness and softness. It also describes the individual who actually mixes the sound levels.

Moratorium: A) A ban on having a guest return to a show, usually for bad behavior. B) An exclusive agreement between a guest and a show not to do any other appearances until their show airs.

MOS: A) This can mean Man on Street; a series of the questions that they ask any "Joe" or "Jane" coming out of a movie theater a grocery store on their opinion on a particular topic. B) "Without sound" and refers to a visual shot that is created without an accompanying soundtrack. The origins of the *"without sound/MOS"* connection are shrouded in legend. Allegedly, when German movie directors came to Hollywood in the Golden Era (as so very many talented men did), they often wanted to shoot *without sound,* which they pronounced as *mit out sound,* hence the term MOS. But in fact, MOS stands for *motor only sync,* a process whereby the camera is run, but the soundtrack is not recording. This was done to save on sound stock for shots that would be dubbed with sound in post-production. Personally, I like the *mit out sound* story better. As the famous line from *The Man Who Shot Liberty Valance* goes, "When the legend becomes fact, print the legend."

NTSC: An acronym for National Television System Committee. The NTSC sets television and video standards in the United States. So an NTSC videotape is playable only in the U.S. Europe and the rest of the world use the PAL system, which is vastly more popular. This means that if you buy a copy of *The Sopranos* in the UK, it won't play on your NTSC VHS player back at home.

One-Sheet: Part of your press kit, a one-sheet is a single page that summarizes the event, news story, or specialty that you wish to pitch to TV producers and includes the who, what, where, when, how, and why.

Opening Graphics: A show's opening graphics, from its logo to its signature visual introduction (think *The Late Show with David Letterman*'s prowl through the nocturnal NYC streets or *Survivor*'s visual survey of distant locales and dangerous tasks).

Option: An option is a legally binding but temporary agreement between two parties that allows the option's purchaser (a studio, production company or individual) to shop around the option seller's product (book; script; life's story). Option money is not always significant. Taking out an option is a way of hedging the purchaser's bet if that party does not wish to buy the property outright. Option fees can be as low as one dollar (as was the case when author Stephen King optioned his novel *Desperation)* or as high as a few hundred thousand dollars. Options also differ widely in terms of length. An option can be for three weeks, three months or three years (any number will do). Word of advice: if you want to option your life's story, the longer the term of the option is, the higher a fee you should negotiate. You don't want beans for a three-year option, for example.

Outro: When a host brings you onstage, he or she will introduce you by telling the studio audience who you are and what you are about. An outro is the opposite proposition, in which a host will repeat key information as well as add in any contact information that has been agreed upon (your PO box or Internet address, for example). You need to know how the producers have scripted your intro and your outro, because promoting yourself or your product or service is all the payment you will receive. Do not trust in others to get this information right: check up on it yourself. Don't be shy now; you have every right to know how we are going to present you!

Permits: A written license granted by an authority. Even a student filmmaker is not supposed to shoot on a city street without a permit. At least, not for any amount of time! A professional production will have every permit required by law. You do not need to worry about this unless you plan to shoot tape for your reel in a public space.

Pictures: Most hosts will happily pose for photographs with all their guests at an appointed time. This is one of the perks for appearing on TV. You need to bring your own camera, or a disposable camera, as not many shows are equipped with their own still photographer. But you must first ask permission from a member of the production staff before snapping a photo with Regis or Alex or Ellen.

Pitch: To present an idea or proposal in a concise verbal format. Usually associated with high pressure situations, but you needn't worry. Just relax, people, and use all the advice I have given to you in this book. You'll do fine! Remember that producers and production staff listen to pitches all day long from a variety of sources, including each other. So they will more or less know right away if they like or need your pitch. That means you should keep it short, keep it simple, and keep it interesting. Just stick with the core concept or idea. If a producer asks for more detail, then flesh things out, *but not too much.* Brevity is the best possible pitching strategy. And never take it personally when somebody turns down your pitch. You don't say yes to every request that comes your way, do you? There is always another show to pitch to, or another hook/angle to cook up that transforms your pitch into something fresh again.

PL: Short for party line, the networked radio communication headset systems used by the producers, director, stage manager, and crew to talk to each other during the taping of the show. Lots of chatter on the PL: some jocularity, but mostly serious business.

Playback: A pretaped video segment or any visual material that has been brought to the taping ahead of time, such as a guest's home movie. When you see clips from previous shows, this is a playback. At home, you'll see a seamless cut from a host or guest to the footage, but the studio audience watches the material on studio monitor screens. The show's associate director cues all playback material.

PO: Short for purchase order. Line producers or production coordinators deal with all matters relating to purchases and rentals.

Postmortem: The meeting that happens with a show staff and crew after the taping to discuss what went wrong, what went right, and what needs to change.

Postproduction: This is the period immediately *after* the shoot (taping), during which a finished show is assembled from raw camera footage. Camera angles are chosen and cut together, graphics and music are added, then the end result is mixed to balance sound levels (audience cheering vs. soft-spoken guest, etc.).

Postproduction Supervisor: Supervises every stage of postproduction, during which a show is assembled and finished.

Preempted: A show can be preempted by local or national news programming if breaking news is happening (a tornado, a presidential speech, a car chase). If the show you have appeared on gets pre-empted in your area, there is no guarantee when it will be aired. That decision is a local one: check local network affiliates for rebroadcast dates.

Pre-Interview: On some shows, you'll get booked based on your materials (press kit, show reel, pitch and hooks), then you will be pre-interviewed so a producer can get a good sense of what you are like and how you will perform. In this case, the pre-interview helps the producer fashion a script for your segment. I prefer a second method, in which the pre-interview is my way of sounding you out and judging whether or not to book you. My pre-interviews are like auditions. I'm not just gauging your answers to questions about your specialty, I'm evaluating other cues like temperament, sense of humor, energy level, or the ability to speak on the fly.

Preproduction: The preproduction phase encompasses everything up to the taping (making) of a show. Due to television schedules, I can be in preproduction on one show, shooting another few episodes, and shepherding another through postproduction. From my point of view, the phases all run concurrently (and sometimes chaotically), but from your vantage point the chain of events will be simple and clear!

Press Kit: A collection of materials which helps "sell" a person or company. They must contain a one-sheet, a bio, press clippings, and show reel.

Press Release: Information, usually taking the form of a faxed or emailed "article," that provides where-when-what-why details for an event or individual. You can create your own press releases and use them in your press kit. The press does not actually have to have received or acknowledged your release, so don't worry, just keep your document punchy, to the point, and interesting!

Private 1: Walkie-talkie lingo for a private one-on-one conversation. Two individuals on opposite ends of the set can have a Private 1 if they switch to a pre-designated non-public frequency.

Prod: An abbreviation for *production,* which is a formal way of referring to a show. We don't actually say *prod,* as this might be taken the wrong way (*"Prod who? Is that like a probe? What?!"*), but it is used as written shorthand.

Producer: A person who supervises, organizes and/or creates a television show (or radio program, or motion picture). There are many different types of producers, as outlined in chapter 2.

Production Manager: She who gets the checks signed! A vital budgetary overseer who keeps track of expenditures and costs. Works in tandem with a show's line producer.

Production Meeting: A meeting in which production staff goes over a show's script with the director and key crew members. The structure of a show is planned: who enters from what side or the stage, etc., and at what precise time confetti will drop from the ceiling if need be.

Production Supplies: Markers, pens, cues cards, blue cards, clipboards, etc. Small but absolutely vital materials!

Props: Anything from a giant beach ball to an ice cream cone that is required for a segment. Also, anything that a guest handles: that book you've written and are publicizing is a prop when it is on a television set.

Public Relations: The business of utilizing the media to convey information about a client, whether an individual or a company, to the public. For more about this subject, see chapter 7.

Publicist: An individual who specializes in using PR techniques to promote their client via any and all media. A publicist can help get you booked on a show. You can also act as your own do-it-yourself publicist. See the amazing and indispensable chapter 7.

Ratings: The be-all and end-all of any television show or network. Ratings are an estimation of what percentage of the viewing public is watching a television (or radio) program. Various companies, such as the Nielsen Media Research, use survey systems to estimate out how many people are watching a show and, more importantly, what that audience's demographic (age, sex, race, etc.) is. The "young" demographic (16–32) is prized due to their free-ranging spending habits, which is why so many television shows seem to cater to this age group. Television is first and foremost a business. Networks charge fees to advertisers (sponsors) based on ratings. A highly rated show such as the Super Bowl will command huge fees per minute of advertising. An infomercial broadcast after midnight will command a vastly smaller fee. No matter how great a TV show is, if it does not get solid ratings it will get cancelled.

Reel or Tape: No, these words do not refer to fishing or gift-wrapping, but rather to your show reel or demo reel used as part of your press kit (see chapter 5).

Releases: A release is a contract by which you give permission for your image to be broadcast to the public. For example, if a TV crew filmed you slipping on a banana peel, then broadcast it on *Conan O'Brien* without your written consent in the form of a signed release, you could sue the pants off the show in question. Not that Conan's people would ever do such a thing. See the appendix for a sample release form.

Remote: Any segment that is taped or broadcast live from a "remote" location, even if the place is just across the street. When a host presents a pre-recorded clip of himself talking to people on the street, this is a remote clip too.

Repeats: Each local network affiliate buys and schedules their own day-time television shows. They repeat shows that they still own broadcast rights to. Repeats are also scheduled when a show is on production hiatus and no new episodes have been planned or made yet. The network affiliates won't award a time slot for a show that's on hiatus to another show because they usually want their audiences to associate that slot with the primary show.

Ring Down: A phone line that connects the booth, where the director is stationed, with the Producer's Table on the set's floor. Instead of ringing, a light on the phone blinks. Used for private communications.

Rundown: The director's version of a script, featuring stage directions as they relate to segment/story beats.

SAG: The Screen Actors Guild. With twenty branches nationwide, SAG represents nearly 120,000 actors in film, television, commercials, and music videos. It has many branches nationwide and is not in the least limited to LA and NYC. The Guild is a collective bargaining entity that negotiates on behalf of its members, and ensures they have fair and equitable working conditions, compensation and benefits. SAG is a proud affiliate of the AFL-CIO.

Satellite: A satellite is any object that orbits another object, which means that your loyal pet pooch technically qualifies. But for our purposes, a satellite is a communications device that is positioned in Earth's upper orbit. These devices can send and receive broadcast signals from anywhere in the world, making it possible for a reporter in London to deliver live coverage of an event to a U.S.-based newscast. Satellites have also been at the root of the global cell phone boom. Satellites are also used to broadcast television content. DirectTV beams digital quality programming directly into your house.

Screening: To view a motion picture or television program. Critics screen movies and TV shows prior to their official release so that timely reviews can be published. Essentially, this is a fancy professional word for "I saw a movie." You will not *screen* your television appearance until it is broadcast in your area.

Screenplay: A blueprint text for a motion picture that contains dialogue and descriptions of action and setting. *Teleplay* is the same thing but for television movies or episodes. You've probably read about the bartender or chiropractor or convenience store clerk who sold his screenplay for one million dollars. It's rare, but it happens.

Script: Although it might seem odd, most unscripted television shows are scripted in advance. When a news anchor reads from a teleprompter, she's reading a prepared script. When you appear as a guest on a television show, your scripted "dialogue" will be agreed upon in advance between you and the production staff. This does not mean that you have to learn any lines! You just have to know what is expected of you in the segment, and we need to decide how you will answer them based on your pitch and point of view.

Scripted Programming: Sitcoms, dramas, and non-reality-based shows are considered scripted programming. The content and nature of this book deals with unscripted programming.

Segment: Each news or talk or reality show is broken down into *segments* divided up by commercial breaks. A show like *Maury Povich* may have as many as six segments per one-hour show. Each segment is scripted by the production staff so that everybody knows where to move and what to talk about. See the entry for script.

Set Designer: A key crewmember who designs a show's set and visual look, in addition to any extra objects that might be needed for a show.

Shooter: A cameraman in the field. As in, "We need to send a shooter out to Weehawken, New Jersey, to cover the pie-eating contest."

Shooting Draft: See final draft.

Shop: Aka "show." As in "Dr. Phil's shop" = "Dr. Phil's show."

Slate: A) An opening graphic on a demo reel or master tape that provides crucial identification or contact information. Your show reel *must* have such a slate, or it will get lost in the shuffle! B) a *slate* of shows is a contractually specified number of programs that must be delivered by a show's production staff to a network or studio. Once a slate has been completed, a show and its staff may go on hiatus for a weeks or months, which means that if you try to contact them to pitch yourself, they will be on vacation in Tahiti (or visiting their in-laws in Yonkers).

Slug: An abbreviated title that describes a topic like "Titanic Sinks!" or "Mom Trapped in Elevator Gives Birth to Healthy Baby."

Sound Bites: A sound bite is a short, quotable segment of film or video. In preparation for a television appearance, you should rehearse yourself by scripting out sound bites or your own. Your show reel should contain an edited series of your TV appearances with an eye towards memorable sound bites. "I'll be back" from the motion picture *The Terminator* is a classic movie sound bite.

Sponsor: An entity, usually a company or other organization, that buys advertising time on a show. So advertisers sponsor the shows they buy time on. The term also includes a more formal and participatory relationship.

Stage Shoot: Any shoot or taping that takes place on a studio sound stage. A *location shoot* is a shoot or taping that takes place anywhere other than a studio, whether exterior (a theme park) or interior (a museum).

Star Trailers: Mobile trailers that have multiple functions. They can be used as a green room for talent, or for costume crew or makeup artists. Also see Honey Wagons.

Sticks: Crew lingo for *tripod,* a three-legged brace atop which a camera is attached. Usually used on location shoots.

Stills: Another word for photograph. A show may make use of *stills* as well as moving images. For example, we may show a clip from a birthday party, then cut to a still photograph of the birthday celebrant on her first birthday. You should be prepared to provide any relevant still photographs to enhance your TV appearance. A member of the production staff will let you know what is needed in advance of your scheduled appearance. Example: if you lost three hundred pounds by eating nothing but grass and nuts, you'll need to show a TV audience a still of your old, hefty-sized self as a visual aide. It's the same principle as show and tell from primary school.

Story By: A movie credit that indicates who came up with a basic story, when others have written the actual screenplay or teleplay.

Sun Gun: A small, hand-held lighting apparatus used to throw extra light onto a moving source, usually a person. A member of the camera crew (standing out of camera range) may use a sun gun to illuminate you as you walk from backstage to front stage. Sun guns can also be mounted to the top of cameras, especially when they are following people on the street or down corridors where studio lights cannot reach.

Table Read: A table read is when the key crew and talent gather together to read through a show (or movie's) script. In my world, the producers may meet separately with the show director and the host, but they will both read through the same script and offer feedback.

Talent: Description for the host, band members, or any celebrity guests. Even the woman who gestures to the merchandise on *The Price is Right* is described as talent. The phrase *"Talent in the house"* indicates that a host or celebrity guest has arrived in the studio, therefore signifying that shoot or taping is soon set to begin gearing up.

Talk-Down: The meeting a producer has with the director and the crew before the show in which they discuss from A to Z how the show or segment is going to be technically and physically executed.

Tape Op: Short for tape operator. During a shoot or taping, each camera produces tapes that have time code numbers (like a VCR counter) printed at the bottom. It is also the tape op's job to synchronize all the time codes, thus making the cameras' points of view all play *"in harmony."* This is all very technical, so don't lose sleep if it sounds complicated or high tech.

Tape Spine: This is the edge of a VHS cassette or cassette box that would face outwards if you filed tapes as a library does (which is what most of us do at home anyway). The spine of a VHS tape you rent from a video shop will have the movie's name written on it. When you send your press kit and show reel to a show's production office, it is essential that you attach a sticker to the tape's spine (cassette and cassette box) detailing your name and phone number. In a busy production office, an unmarked demo reel will get lost in the shuffle in no time flat. Those of you with small children in daycare or school will be familiar with the idea of writing your child's name on everything from socks to underwear. The same goes for your show reel!

Taped: Ninety-nine percent of news and talk TV is produced via a video taping process. TV sitcoms are usually taped. Dramas often use film, which has a superior quality, but is vastly more expensive than tape. The rise of digital systems, which are also low cost, will equalize the budgetary gulf between tape and film, and will replace both formats.

Technical Director: Responsible for switching the camera shots that the director calls. Acts in tandem with the Tape Op to create the line cut, a rough assembly of footage used as a guide in the postproduction-editing phase.

Telecine: This is a process that transfers film to video. If a producer asks you to send in home movies that are on Super8, you will have to get them telecined onto VHS tape for two reasons. A) Super8 projectors are extremely rare in this day and age and NO production office will have one, and B) you want to copy original materials that can get lost in the mail (or at a production office).

Traffic: The network that owns a show handles all advertising placement traffic, commercial breaks within the show's time format, as well as between one show and the next. If producers had to handle this complicated job too, we'd never sleep and never get to go home.

Transfer: To make a copy (aka dub) or a tape, or to translate from one format to another. For example, motion picture movies are *transferred* to DVD and video so that you can play them on your home entertainment system.

Unions: An organization that bargains for a collective number of individuals, to advance its member's interests. Most television shows can only use crew people who are members of their respective profession's union. For example, if your fairy godmother waved her magic wand and turned you into a television host with your own show, you'd still have to join

SAG in order to have your show broadcast. Not even magical powers can circumvent union contacts with a studio or network. Unions protect their members from being taken advantage of: if they work overtime, they get paid overtime, etc.

Unscripted Programming: All reality-based television shows that are not of the sitcom and drama world. The nature of this book is about becoming a guest on unscripted television shows.

Voiceover: A voiceover is a narration that is played over a film or video segment. Documentaries and news programs use lots of voiceover (aka VO), as do commercials and movie trailers. *Voiceover Artists* specialize in narrating radio and television commercials: as performers, they are represented by SAG, the Screen Actor's Guild.

Walkie Talkie: A small, portable communications device that broadcasts and receives a variety of radio frequencies. Used by production staff and crew on a shoot or taping. CB radios are distant cousins to Walkie Talkies, the main difference being that you can't walk around and talk with a CB set up.

Wrap: The end of a show.

Wrap Around: A section of a show that is taped separately from the body of the shoot or taping in which guests and a studio audience are involved. A wrap around might be used as an intro for a special episode or a "best of..." clip show.

If we're missing anything here shoot us an email with the definition and we'll add it to the list.

www.JacquieJordan.com

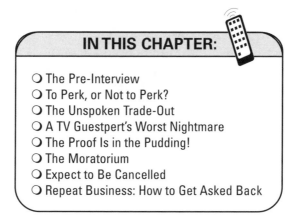

Chapter 9

Booked, Bumped, or Cancelled: What to Do and How to Behave

IN THIS CHAPTER:

○ The Pre-Interview
○ To Perk, or Not to Perk?
○ The Unspoken Trade-Out
○ A TV Guestpert's Worst Nightmare
○ The Proof Is in the Pudding!
○ The Moratorium
○ Expect to Be Cancelled
○ Repeat Business: How to Get Asked Back

The Pre-Interview

Producers book guests on television through a standard process called the pre-interview, which is done by phone. Some producers may book you and then set up a time for a pre-interview. Other producers, in my opinion the majority, will call and pre-interview you *before* they commit to booking you, especially if you have not made any or many television appearances. I choose this latter process. Think of it like this: you are the car and I am a potential buyer. I am going to kick your tires and take you for a test drive before making a commitment to you.

It bears repeating: a producer stakes their reputation on you when they book you and put you on air. If you seize up in the middle of a taping, it's my fault! I need to both know who you are *and how you are* before I take the chance putting you on the air.

If you've followed the previous chapters, then this is the part of the process that you have been waiting for—to get on TV. I am assuming that all the groundwork has been laid: you have built a media platform, made a press kit, etc. This preparation has been time-consuming, but here is where it pays off, and a producer finally books you on the show of your dreams (or simply one that you have targeted). As the saying goes, it can take a few years to become an overnight sensation!

The process goes like this: you've pitched to the show producer, who has reviewed your materials and was impressed. A basic "Hello, how are you?" phone or email relationship has been established. The countdown to blast off has hopefully begun, but here comes the final hurdle: the pre-interview.

Think of a pre-interview as an audition that happens over the phone. Although it may feel like a casual, shooting the breeze chat about you and your product/story/pitch, it most certainly is not. I am carefully gauging several factors at once. You are in the spotlight here and you must come through. This is your big moment to shine, and it is just as important as that hoped for televised appearance.

I may call up with disappointing news: we may be booked solid until next year. You have been bumped before even getting booked. But in this conversation, I am still auditioning you. How do you handle the unexpected? How do you deal with cancellation and disappointment?

Or let's say that I make a spontaneous decision to call you on your cell phone, thus increasing the likelihood that you are out and about, doing errands, picking up screaming kids from school, rushing out work deadlines, and so on. I'm sorry to put you on the spot here, but again, you response is being evaluated. Do you communicate clearly while under pressure? How low is your annoyance threshold? Get your game face on, pardners, because that ringing phone may be your lucky break, and you have to perform with grace and style. There are almost no "do-overs." High energy is what we producers are looking for from a guest; we want to know that you contain the potential for a few minutes of great television.

So just know that a casual phone call from me or another producer is part of a critical decision making process, which will indicate whether or not I want to pursue having another conversation with you.

If I do decide to book you for a show, it will be because I have faith in your pitch and materials, and enough confidence in you to sell you to the rest of my staff. I am selling you to them without you being present. They are taking me at my word.

Let's circle back to the pre-interview. I call you up, I have some ideas, I'm kind of sort of feeling you out, and I will be trying to pull out a point of view from you. Return to our "Marriage Makes You Fat" hook, around which I am planning a show segment. I'm trying to book a relationship therapist (your hypothetical specialty) who says that's absolutely ridiculous. If I knock on your door, my point of view will be—"Marriage makes you fat, well what do you think about that?" I'll want to know what you will and won't say on the subject. How far can you take your criticism and rebuttal? I know *exactly what I want from you.* Why? Because I've written a script for the show before I've actually cast the "role" of the relationship therapist. If you feel that you cannot play this "role," that's absolutely fine. Saying "No" does not count against you at all, *unless you refuse to back up what's in your press kit.* If I call you because you state "X" in your materials ("Marriage makes you thin," for instance), but you refuse to go on record and back up the statement, then you've been wasting my time all along. Put your money where your mouth is, and don't make claims that you cannot or will not back up!

The flip side of this equation is that even though your specialty is well-represented in television (therapist, diet expert, etc.), producers are always looking for fresh talent and takes from these experts. And if my first pre-interview does not give me the results I am looking for, then I'll call another relationship therapist, and another, and another, until I find the right person that I need for my show. Maybe that person near the end of my call list will be you!

The pre-interview is a serious stage of the game, folks. Treat it with professionalism and you won't go wrong. And do not compromise your integrity just to get booked. If you are not comfortable being "devil's advocate" and criticizing a point of view or issue or product, just say no!

To Perk, or Not to Perk?

Congratulations! You've been booked. You're going to be on TV! Here is a guide to perks and benefits. Rule of thumb: Getting booked on a television show does not equate with winning a jackpot prize! My show's budget may seem high, but every nickel is squeezed tight. You are one of a hundred guests that will appear on my show this season. And as much as I'd like to give spa passes to each and every one of you, the budget will almost always say, "What? Are you nuts! Are we made of money? No!" (Budgets tend to get hysterical when asked for extras.)

Your goal is not just to get booked, but to get booked again. So one basic strategy is: be nice and easy. We producers love working with a low-maintenance, "say what you mean, mean what you say" guest. It pays to leave your ego at home. If it comes down to the end of a show's production cycle and the budget is getting tight, then booking decisions are made strategically on fiscal viability and performance potential. Producers will book a low-maintenance, high-performing guest over the high-maintenance, high-performing guest every time.

Many guests see a car service as a booking perk. After all, shouldn't they get something for donating their time and expertise to the show? Well, here's a rule: Don't expect car service and risk not asking for it. *If it's offered, still don't accept it.*

Huh?

Most production companies prefer not to pay for your car service if you are capable of getting yourself to and from the studio location in one piece. Again, our expenditures for each show may seem high or even excessive from an outside point of view, but we really do run a tight ship. And many producers cannot authorize such extras anyway. There are always channels, people, and we can't order you a masseuse any more than we can cut you a nice fat bonus check for being on our show. Help us out here.

Your goal again is to get booked and booked again, so forgo a few nice perks and manage your own way to the show, so that you are saying that you are easygoing.

Now there is an exception to the "refuse the car" rule. If a producer *insists* on your arrival in a car, then by all means accept it. The producing team has the ability to monitor a guest's arrival via the car service, which they will want to do if the shooting schedule is tight, or traffic is bad at that time of day. Producers can check in with a car service and receive messages of "guest ten minutes out" or "guest five minutes out." The producers thus have a sense of relief and control knowing that you are in a vehicle that they can keep close tabs on. In this kind of situation, car service is a necessity, and not a perk.

NEWS FLASH

Don't arrive too early or too late. Although it would seem logical that arriving early is a safe bet, in fact it creates problems, as space is at a premium on the set. If you come before the producers expect you, they may not have room for you, and tending to your comfort will throw off the staff's schedule on their most hectic day. Just show up on time. We won't ask you to turn up at ten a.m. and put you in front of a camera at ten-fifteen! There will be time for you to prepare yourself for your appearance and walk though the script for your segment with a producer.

We'll cover precisely what happens between your arrival and your segment in chapter 10.

The Unspoken Trade-Out

Sometimes, you will get booked, go on a show, and everything will be just as you imagined it might be. The host will ask all the questions you expected in regards to your story, product, point of view, and so forth. You'll leave the studio knowing that everything has gone according to plan, that the audience knows everything it needs to know and more about you and your content. But prepare yourself: there will be days and bookings that are quite different.

We've already talked about how producers cast experts or guests in accordance with a script that has been written in advance of any actual bookings. If my script does not match your platform or mission statement, then just let it go. I may come back to you. Don't make promises that you feel uncomfortable keeping. Be flexible, but don't be a pushover. The last thing in the world a producer would want is for you to regret an appearance on one of our shows. You are our *guest* in every sense of the world. We want you to go away happy.

If you do agree to the parameters established in my script and the pre-interview we share, there is the unspoken trade-out factor. The trade out goes like this: you come onto our show, fit your pitch to our general scripted (pre-planned) requirements, and, in essence, do your thing our way. In exchange, you will get a plug on national television. Your plug will be for a book or a website or an event. That's the trade-out, that's how this works. And if you have built a solid platform with the potential base of ancillaries then this trade-out is invaluable.

Manager and brand visionary Angelica Holiday calls this "Dialing for Dollars." She says, "I booked a client on *Regis and Kathie Lee* and it was a lot of work for him to deliver the six minutes, including being very expensive. He had to fly himself to New York, pay for the hotel room, and for everything used in the segment. But, in the end, the air time was worth $300K to him because he had done the preliminary leg work in building his platform."

Please don't misunderstand: we won't be calling you up to ask you to act out of character. Whatever we have scripted will have significant over-laps with your mission statement. We're calling you because you fit the bill for what we need. The fit may not be perfect and you may of course decline the invitation for a booking. In order to create great TV, we pro-ducers have to leave nothing to chance! You'll get the chance to be spon-taneous within the confines of our scripts. Don't worry: we won't saddle you with a dull role. It's all good fun.

You do have every right to know how we plan to present you. Ask ques-tions, satisfy your curiosity, allay any doubts you may be harboring. There are a few things you will need to know in order to accept a trade out in your booking. The trade-out is what you've been working towards by building a platform. You will want an inherent plug for your book, web-site, company, location—it's the "what you get out of being on TV." The producer gets to sell their segment with your participation to their audi-ence with a met expectation. In order to protect and guarantee you will get your plug, the following checklist is a list of questions you will want to ask your producer.

- How will I be introduced?
- How will the show plug my book or website or event?
- How will the show visually show my book or website? Full screen-graphic or prop?
- What will my introductory on-screen graphics (aka chyrons or lower-thirds) look like and how will they read?
- How will the show handle my follow-up? (In other words, once you've deliv-ered your content, how will the host follow-up and give you one last plug?) Can I link my website to the show's website? Will the host give out my infor-mation (address, phone number, Internet address) directly to viewers?
- What are the beats (main informational points) to my segment?
- How long will my segment be?
- When will my segment air?
- Can I get a copy of my segment?

A TV Guestpert's Worst Nightmare

In the next chapter, I'll share with you a producer's worse nightmare, but first, the following story is a TV guestpert's worse nightmare, and it happened to the one man you wouldn't want it happening to because he was the TV writer for the *Los Angeles Times* and is now the chief TV critic for *Variety,* which means he gets to write about his TV experiences in the newspaper. Brian Lowry recounted his experience in an article he wrote after he was booked on FOX's *The O'Reilly Factor* to talk about *Frogmen*, an NBC pilot starring O.J. Simpson that miraculously failed to surface even in the exploitative aftermath of the Simpson trial. As Brian wrote in his article: "Assuming a guest had dropped dead or failed to show up, I was seated across from O'Reilly, who told me the breathtaking news: Donna Hanover, the wife of Mayor Rudolph Giuliani, had held a press conference saying her husband had cheated on her and that they were going to separate. Desperate for any angle to get into the story, O'Reilly wanted to explore if there would be a lot of media coverage of this latest development."

Not the subject that Brian was booked to speak about or briefed to speak about. In a conversation with Brian, he said, "He tap-danced through it, but ultimately, he could have lost his job as he's not a political commentator." Brian fired off at the producer after the show and said that he would never appear on that show again. O'Reilly called and apologized for the show's last-minute switcheroo of topics.

What do you do in a situation that comes up like that? Brian handled it with great professionalism and candor: "Tap-dancing as best I could, I pointed out the story would undoubtedly get a lot of attention. News coverage, I suggested, often breaks down into what is interesting and what is relevant, and this fell into the former category if not the latter.... After what seemed like an eternity of this blather, O'Reilly made a rather awkward transition to the topic that I had nearly forgotten brought me there in the first place, *Frogmen*. He misidentified who currently holds the rights to the project and asked whether I felt it should be put on now—a question that really had nothing to do with the story I wrote, which was all about what happened a half-dozen years ago and the experiences of those involved."

It is your prerogative to walk off the set. If you are put in the situation as Brian was while you are already in the chair, you answer the questions only from the knowledge base in which you speak of as Brian did by pointing at that the Giuliani incident would attract media attention and he explained why. Given Brian's expertise of being a writer for newspapers, he understands what is news. However, the situation is still awkward for all, and in the end—no one wins out from circumstances like this.

The Proof Is in the Pudding!

You've just made your first appearance on *Popular Show X,* but none of your friends and family were able to view or tape your fabulous debut. How do you prove that you were on television? The answer is simple: just ask the show's producers for a copy of your segment.

It is absolutely the producer's job to give their guest a copy of the show or the segment in which they've appeared after it's aired. However, we producers are often too busy, too overwhelmed, or have moved too far forward to do so in a timely fashion. We aren't the keepers of the show's master tapes and we don't usually have access to the postproduction dubbing facility (where copies are made). Those postproduction folks might be overwhelmed themselves. And sometimes management might discourage the practice of dubbing tapes as this reduces the costs of tape stock, postproduction time, and postage. A TV guest's entitlement to a copy of his or her appearance can sometimes get lost in the shuffle. And yet, this material is crucial for updating your press kit. You *need* a copy, just as we all need a paycheck in exchange for work performed.

Now, producers understand their obligation to providing you with fresh material for your press kit. You will get your dubbed copy of your show or segment in the end. On the positive side, I have worked on shows that have the dubbing system worked out to perfection so that a guest walks out the door with a tape, hot off the presses, so to speak. But on the minus side, there are overburdened production staff who mean well, but will be very late in fulfilling their obligation. Now I will usually tape a show in my office in order to ensure a guest gets their copy, but when things get hectic again—and things are *always* getting hectic again—good intentions can quickly be forgotten. Plus, me taping it off of TV is not the best quality version that you need.

The best approach is to keep the gears well oiled by being as helpful and solicitous as possible with the relevant producer. After your appearance, send a thank-you card along with a blank, pre-labeled VHS tape and a self-addressed, stamped envelope. No producer, no matter how harried, will be able to ignore such a polite and thorough gesture.

To be frank, your best bet as far as insurance goes is to have a back-up plan: have a trusted friend tape your appearance. Somebody with access to a digital television service is the best bet for a clean copy. If a postproduction facility burns to the ground along with the only master tape of your appearance, you'll be happy that you made your own arrangements!

The Moratorium

Moratoriums are lists of "no go" guests or experts. There are ways in which you can be temporarily banned or permanently blackballed. So behave, people! One guest was banned from a studio that oversaw several shows because she was what is called a "media whore." She takes every opportunity to go on TV and say whatever a producer needs her to say and it contradicts what she's said on other shows.

We may also ask for a voluntary moratorium from you. This means that we value your uniqueness so much, the freshness of your approach, that we do not really want you popping up on somebody else's show using the same hook you had on our show. Think of it in terms of exclusivity. We book you and as a condition of that booking, we ask that you do not make another television appearance until your segment has aired. Our show may tape many episodes at once. If you then get booked on another show, your later appearance might get aired before the former. Then we'll feel all "Johnny come lately" even though we found you first!

If you are contacted by another show after having agreed to a moratorium, just tell them thanks, but no thanks. Explain the agreement you have made with our show, and offer the second show a handful of different hooks on your pitch that they might use in future. Television is a small world, so be careful not to burn any bridges by violating moratorium agreements. Word gets around!

Expect to Be Cancelled

What to do when you get booked? Expect to get cancelled!

Although this may sound like a cliché: *don't take it personally.* Topical shows that broadcast daily and are reliant on the shifting tides of current events can be particularly unpredictable.

In 2002–03, I worked with Anthony V. Salerno (see chapter 5) as a media consultant for six months. We had just launched a timely publicity blitz to get him booked on topical news shows at for the Winona Ryder shoplifting trial and the infamous Robert Blake murder case.

Our timing couldn't have been better. By the time we got the press kits and demo reel tapes out, Winona's trial had been postponed just long enough for us to start making the appropriate follow-up phone calls. Even the trial's unpredictable start date worked in our favor.

Our first booking for Anthony was to be on *Celebrity Justice,* which we declined. The segment that he was being booked for wouldn't have highlighted his strengths as a defense attorney, and because he was a rookie, we needed to establish his brand right away. We said no to this particular trade-out.

The second booking was for Court TV's *Catherine Crier Show.* Now that was hitting the mother lode! Unbelievable. We got right down to the wire on this one. The satellite link-up location was picked and the interview time was set. Anthony was going to be on TV for the opening day of the Winona Ryder case.

And then, as all too often, his booking got cancelled. The *Catherine Crier* producer explained that they didn't think enough was going to happen on the first day to warrant Anthony's appearance, and that they would consider booking him later in the week. They did cover the trial as planned, but without Anthony. So even if you are sitting in the makeup room prior to taping a show, things can go wrong. Again: do not take cancellations personally. They happen *all the time.*

Very soon after the cancellation, Anthony Salerno began to pop like popcorn. He was a featured guest on Court TV, CNN, FOX (local and national), *Celebrity Justice* (a different segment), and has since been booked multiple times on *Catherine Crier.*

The key reason as to why he got booked is that he handled the cancellation well. He didn't bitch and moan about how he changed his schedule around. He kept in touch with the producers and was grateful for the opportunity.

Repeat Business: How to Get Asked Back

There is no trick or gimmick or magic rule here. On a basic level, you will get asked back only when we need you again! But to insure the best possible chances of our picking you and not another person with your specialty, just follow the guidelines in this chapter.

- Be polite. Don't be pushy, don't tell us how to do our jobs or what the best way is to sell you.
- Be a low-maintenance guest. Getting booked on TV does not mean that you can suddenly behave like an A-list diva!
- Deliver the goods as promised. If you promise to take a position on an issue, you just follow through.
- Be flexible. Your first few TV appearances might not be ideal. You may have to take a trade-out that does not highlight your mission statement or product in the best possible manner. You may be playing second stringer. Be patient. Good things come to those who wait!
- Honor moratorium requests. If you promise to keep your latest hook under wraps until we broadcast your segment, do so.
- Be professional. Don't expect us to deliver everything to you on a platter. *Ask questions as they relate to your planned appearance.* Show a keen interest in how we plan to present you on our show.

- Be upbeat. Don't get all moody and bummed out if we cancel you! It really does happen all the time and we will do our best to use you again ASAP.
- Try sending a thank-you card! That's an inside tip. Out of the ten thousand guests I've booked, I've received *ten* thank-you notes! Did you make all that effort to do a show, get a tape copy, and go home? No! Send a thank-you note or card. It's such a small effort. Besides look at the investment you've made in getting there...a thank-you card is as invaluable as that postcard you sent. You want to come back, don't you?

From the pre-interview to the booking to the sometimes cancellation, this process is like a roller coaster ride filled with ups and downs. But if you've done your early work, developed your hooks, practiced your pitch, built your platform, then this part of the TV game should be exciting and fruitious because once you are booked, then it's literally showtime and all I can pause to say here is "break a leg."

Chapter 10

It's Showtime: How to Float "On Air"

This is the chapter that is the marriage between what you have worked so hard to obtain and with what we do happens. And we've finally found each other and we're ready to make sweet TV magic together! Figuratively speaking, it's time for you to walk out onto that stage set, face the cameras, and be on air.

A Producer's Worst Nightmare

Actually, this was my worst nightmare: a live, on-the-air meltdown. This is the worst possible potential disaster. At least a botched segment on a taped show can be edited down or even dropped entirely. Mercifully, the crisis in question was averted by intervention from the most unexpected of sources. This is a tale of true grace under pressure.

Back in last decade's dot-com boom, the *Wall Street Journal* and I.T.T. briefly owned a New York City television station called WBIS+. I was a segment producer for a two-hour live show called *Money, Style, Power* (how 1990s is that?). Carol Martin was the host of the program. She's a New York City anchor and personality. Josh Binswanger, now on A&E, was the co-host.

The program was almost totally centered on Manhattan, the famed Big Apple. I read an article in the *New York Times,* where I happened across a great real estate story with a "dreams come true" angle. A married couple bought into a downtown brownstone, initially purchasing just one bedroom. Then, the upstairs units went up for sale, which they snapped up too. Eventually, they were in the position of being able to buy the entire brownstone. This middle-class couple suddenly became property-owning millionaires living the real estate dream in New York City, no less! The hook for the show was *How did they do this? And can you do this too?* Did they set out to buy the entire brownstone when they first started renting it? How did they finance the ever-growing purchases of units? Believe me, this is something that every resident of NYC daydreams about.

I had a potentially rock-solid show segment, but first I had to do a phone pre-interview with the couple. I'd seen their photo in the article, so I knew that they were presentable folks. All I had to do was size them up via a phone chat. As it tuned out, the wife had the proverbial gift of the gab: here was a person who could talk about any subject under the sun and come off as fascinating. Alas, the husband almost literally had nothing to say. He seemed awkward and reticent in his wife's larger-than-life shadow. Because this was the story of a married couple's dream, I needed to include the hubby regardless of his unsuitability for television. I assumed that the wife would carry the segment off with style and panache. How very wrong I was!

The wife and husband arrive. They look good. She is sociable, he is demure: everything as expected. They sit down and Carol Martin starts the interview on cue from the show's stage manager. Remember now, this is a live show, not a live-to-tape show. As of this cue, we are broadcasting on the air and directly into your home. Then, the crisis begins and the show is thrust to the brink of the television abyss. It only takes five seconds or so.

The wife begins rocking back and forth like a mother does as she holds a baby. She starts slowly, begins to look rather ill, and starts to rock a little faster. I feel a heart attack sneaking up behind me. *I've booked a woman with a nervous tick.* She has no sense of body control whatsoever. I felt as though even Carol was getting concerned.

As a producer, I am still completely responsible for the woman's performance because it was my judgment to invite her, even though I had no way of foreseeing this nervous behavior (nor, as it turns out, had the wife ever experienced this reaction before).

The poor woman was bobbing in small, tight circles, like a serpent entranced by a snake charmer! The segment, and my career, was crashing before our very eyes! I felt as though Carol was going to have to dive underneath the wife in order to catch her.

And then, out of nowhere, the husband calmly intervened by jumping right into the interview as if nothing special was happening at all. He was articulate, dynamic, and outspoken. We shot him on close-up as his wife remained in the grips of her unexpected bout of stage fright. *This man saved the day.* Who would have suspected such fortitude from our wishy-washy pre-interview?

When we got off the air, the wife collapsed into my arms, sobbing. She started to cry about what a fool she made on this live show of herself and how her family and coworkers were watching.

The truth is nobody in the world remembers this incident but me, and probably her. Our cameras only caught her stage fright for a minute or two, then we concentrated on our hero of the hour, the husband. Talk about saved by the bell!

Now you probably won't have to perform such a bold rescue on live television—and amongst the ten thousand-plus guests I have booked on TV, this is the one and only time I have had this experience—but the story does serve to illustrate the quality of grace under pressure. The reticent husband stepped up to the plate and took control of the segment on his wife's behalf.

Seven Tips to Help You Perfect Your Performance

I know that some of you are worried about stage fright and the time has now come to take that bull by the horns and wrestle it to the ground. Do you know how many of my multitude of guests have blown a segment due to stage fright? *Almost none.* Producers don't book bad TV guests. It's our job not to. But your appearance counts, because as they say, "You never get a second chance to make a first impression." If you have a doubt in your mind that you are not on-camera savvy, then get yourself ready!

First off, butterflies are normal and necessary, as you'll read later. If you don't feel like you are going to throw up before you go on air, then I will throw up!

But before you can prepare for the outer appearance, you must be internally prepared. As a producer, I am empowering you to know the following secrets for "Perfecting Your Appearance."

TV GUESTPERT'S "PERFECTING YOUR APPEARANCE" MANTRA:

1. When you go on TV, you are *not* being interviewed, you are simply having a conversation. Just as you do every day of your life. You do not need permission to speak, *we want to hear you talk.*

2. The host/guest relationship is *not* like that of teacher/student or parent/child. You are the host's honored guest, a visitor to his or her "home."

3. Remember, the segment is happening because of *you!* Your content is the reason why everybody has gathered in the studio. Without guests there can be no show, no reason for its very existence.

4. Just because five cameras and a studio audience are watching your segment does not mean that anything has changed from the phone pre-interview stage. You were passionate, articulate, and energetic then and you will be passionate, articulate, and energetic on television.

5. Guests get worried about making fools out of themselves, or saying the wrong thing. But the truth is this: *you know your material better than anybody in the studio.*

6. The actual taping is the endpoint of a hard fought campaign on your part. You've built your platform, you've stuck to your mission statement, you've cultivated hooks, developed relationships with a producing staff, and you have *already* sold us on your content. Think of your on air performance as a *party in your honor* for all your dedication and determination. You've run the gauntlet and you've got past the hard part!

7. Nerves are normal, nerves are natural, nerves are a *good* thing. If you are not nervous, then I get nervous, because nervousness translates to energy on screen.

Write them down and keep them in your pocket for handy reassurance if need be. And trust me, I've been doing this for over ten years: you will be fine!

Arrival

Let me set the scene: you've taken your comped flight to the city where the show you've been booked on is taping. Although you are very, very excited, you have foregone socializing or late afternoon sightseeing, and are fast asleep at a respectable hour. You awaken bright and fresh-faced and are ready for your official television debut.

The show's producers did not offer you car service. And you would have declined it anyway, right? Unless they insisted (see chapter 9). You step outside of your hotel and get into a taxicab.

Upon your arrival at the studio set, a production assistant or associate producer will meet and greet you. The environment may seem bustling and busy and you may feel out of place, but rest assured, you are a vital and important part of our show. We know it, even if we are too frantic to let you know!

What to Bring with You

What do you bring to the studio? Yourself, obviously, dressed in appropriate clothing. Bring two additional wardrobes. You may look fabulous in what you were wearing, but the host could be wearing the same thing. They'll ask you to change because the host has already taped three segments of the show in her outfit. Changing now would throw off show continuity, so you'll be the one inconvenienced. Think about your wardrobe choices in advance, although don't stress out too much. Talk to your producer about options. Take digital pictures in your outfits. Get your producer's feedback. I always have final say on what my guests wear and I like to decide in the green room based on the colors that have been worn in other segments. Remember, you are going to be on TV, not dining with the Queen of England.

It's not about what your best color is, it's about what color looks best on camera.

TV CLOTHING RULES:

- No white—it throws off color balance.
- No all black—there is no depth in the picture.
- No white and black together—they are too contrasting for color balance.
- No busy prints—they might blur together.
- No stripes—they will start to move in the picture.
- Solid bright colors look best. Reds, bright blues, shades of green.

Business casual is the standard. If you are a slightly zany child psychologist or teacher, then loud print shirts are fine. If you are a musician or any sort of hipster, dress as you would on any day of the week, but make an effort not to appear scruffy—wear your newest T-shirt and sneakers! But no logos. It becomes a clearance issue. A camera that is set up for a wide shot will be able to see your ankles and shoes, so make sure your socks are matched and your shoes are polished.

What about makeup and hair? My rule of thumb is to wear your day makeup and hairstyle: whatever cosmetics you usually use each and every day. You should look as you would normally. This isn't the time to try out a new hairstyle. If you don't like it, then you lose your self-confidence to perform. If you have long straight hair, a huge new beehive will be something that the producer will want to know in advance about. We'll talk more about hair and makeup in a subsequent section.

This is the time you bring along that blank, brand new VHS tape and a self addressed stamped manila-style envelope, so that the producer can mail you a clean, professional standard dub copy of the completed show and hand it to your producer when you arrive. Plus, this is probably the first time you meet your producer and associate producer face to face.

Finally, bring along something to occupy your time. A book, magazine, cell phone, laptop: whatever makes you comfortable. One axiom of TV show taping is: hurry up and wait. We want you here right on time, you rush off to make the deadline, then you might wait around for an hour before the taping begins.

Inside the Green Room

After the meet and greet, you will be taken to the green room where you will stay until called for makeup, then later show time.

A *green room* is any backstage space set aside where the performers can wait for their cues. The origins of the term are a part of theatrical folklore upon which no two theories even remotely agree. Nobody really knows where the term came for, or why the rooms are said to be green (they can be any color). The term has been in use since at least the early 1700s, when it was first referenced in print. "The Green" was a medieval term for stage that may have originated from outdoor performances in which the "stage" was covered with grass. Another theory holds that this is the room where the actors got paid—with green money, naturally—but this don't hold water, as most international paper currency is (and has always been) multicolored. Plus, back in 1700, everybody used coins as legal tender. Is it called the green room because green is a soothing color? That take sounds plausible, but also has a hint of twentieth-century psychological theory and retroactive justification: perhaps a case of wishful thinking? Whatever the origins of the term, the green room has a long and illustrious history, one that you are now taking part in.

Did I mention that food and beverages are available in the green room? I thought that'd raise a smile. You need not worry about bringing change for the vending machine. We've got you covered. But don't expect caviar and egg white omelets, please, and please come on a full stomach as it's unlikely you'll be able to eat if you have butterflies in your stomach. And remember, you *should* have butterflies in your stomach.

The associate producer will provide you with release forms to be signed. These forms give the show and network permission to use the footage shot for the show. They reserve certain rights, such as promotional use of your image. For example, they might use an image of you from the show on an official show website, or a clip of your segment for any kind of advertising for the show. This is all standard procedure, so don't worry about all the sternly worded legalese. Read the release form, but rest assured they exist to protect you just as much as to protect us. These release forms are standard. Familiarize yourself with it in the appendix of this book. You can also ask your producer to fax you a release form prior to your appearance so that you have time to read and comprehend it. Be informed ahead of time. We, the producers, will *absolutely* not record any performance with you unless you sign that release form and if you decide to finagle your way around it let me tell you it's *hasta la vista, baby, forever!* See the appendix for Consent and Release forms.

Everyday Makeup and Hair

Each show is different in the way that they prepare for a taping. So after signing your release forms, you may be whisked off to hair and makeup. Then again, you may not. This is where that reading material or laptop that you brought along will come in handy to kill some time.

I have a saying for how best to approach the subject of grooming. Just come in your everyday hair and makeup. The hair and makeup artists will then know what your comfort level is as far as appearance goes. They'll give you makeup that is appropriate for studio TV lighting, but you'll still look like you, not a painted clown, on screen.

Why are there special makeup techniques for TV (and film)? That's due to the aforementioned studio lights, which are bright. If you went on without any makeup at all, you'd look wan and washed out. And all you men who don't wear makeup (hey, I work in L.A.: men wear makeup here), fear not. Our makeup artists might put a little rouge on your cheeks or possibly something on your lips for highlighting, but you will not look like a member of the rock group KISS. The added studio makeup job will totally even out. The effects of the lights and the way in which the cameras "see" balances out the makeup and you'll look perfectly normal. My goal is that you feel your best and look your best. I don't want you to be shocked by what you look like, so give the makeup artist something to work with by wearing your usual style of makeup.

You'd think that I would not have to remind anybody to wash his or her hair, but think again. I have had guests show up without having showered, expecting a fancy shampoo and blow-dry. We are not here to make you over: that's another show format entirely! But we are committed to making you look good, because when you look good, we look good.

The Walk-Through Talk (aka The Briefing)

There you sit in the green room, hair pleasantly coifed, makeup blended perfectly, sipping a soda, snacking on munchies, reading the latest magazine or Grisham thriller. Then a producer will stop by and remind you that yes, this is a TV show taping, not a vacation spa.

A good producer will carefully walk you through your segment and reiterate what was discussed in the pre-interview process. None of this information should be a surprise to you, as you'll have agreed to script requirements in that pre-interview. Think of this walk-through, known as the briefing, as a final dress rehearsal before the curtain rises and the real show begins.

A producer will do the following:

- Tell you what time you will go on stage.
- Tell you how long you will be on stage.
- Talk you through the segment's script and read through the intro that the host will use to introduce you.
- Walk you through the beats (key points) of your segment.
- Tell you how you are expected to respond to the host's questions (again, you will already have a clear idea of this from the pre-interview).
- Show you exactly what your name (and product, book, etc., if relevant) will look like when displayed on screen.

Obviously, you really need to pay attention and take some notes during the pre-interview phase.

I'd like to elaborate on the producer's briefing. We will not tell you what the host's questions will be, as we want you to be as spontaneous as possible within the context of what we have scripted and planned out. But we will go over the major beats of the segment and let you know what the shape and direction of the conversation will be like. Think of this as an A-B-C-D-to-E overview as to how your topic will be discussed. Most prepared producers will *feed back your best sound bites back to you,* the ones you've already developed via your materials, press kit, and through the pre-interview process.

What Does a Script Look Like, Anyway?

I am often asked by guests, usually during the briefing, if they can read a script. I *never* show a guest a script. There are many reasons why I don't do that. Some guests have felt that this was secretive of me, but from experience I have found that when a guest sees a script that is written for the host to execute, it throws them off their intended performance or panics them. Then the conversation becomes about what is written on paper and not on what needs to happen. I've had this struggle with publicists who want "to protect" their clients and demand to see the scripts. I still hold the line here. Plus, the show never turns out exactly verbatim as what happens on the script. Hopefully, it turns out better.

I don't want to be held to what was written in the script for what didn't happen or hold back the potential of what may happen in the moment. Our script is an internal document used to function a show. My concern is to get you off the paper and into a moment. However, I have included a standard script for your review. The briefing is not the time to make demands on seeing the script. I will, however, show you your pre-interview and what you said.

[*Segment #6*
Show Title: Millie Really Talk Show
Producer: Jacquie Jordan
Associate producer: Mark Parsons
TRT: 7:00
TD: 9/25/05   AD: 10/5/05

INTRO	HOST ON CAMERA
Welcome back. Our next guest has helped Las Vegas Show girls lose the weight they gained during their pregnancy in order to regain their dancing figure. Today, he's got a few tricks up his sleeve for us, please welcome Stage Hypnotist Dr. Scott Lewis.	B-ROLL: VEGAS SHOW GIRL WORK OUT VIDEO w/ Guest HELPING SHOW GIRLS CLOSE-UP: GUEST L/3: Scott Lewis, DC, Stage Hypnotist
Scott, Some would consider you lucky, others smart, what's it like helping Vegas Show Girls to lose weight? • After pregnancy anecdote • Explains he's a chiropractor by day and a Vegas show doctor by night, performing at the Riviera.	B-ROLL: Vegas Show Girls L/3: Vegas Show Girl Workout B-ROLL: Scott at his office with patients and Scott at night his show at Riviera
TRANSITION TO AUDIENCE	PROP: HAND HELD MIC
Today Scott is going to help one member of our audience with his techniques he uses to help Vegas Show Girls.	HOST/ AUDIENCE SHOT
INTRO SALLY JENNINS Sally is a pre-qualified, pre-selected audience member and mother of 4, most recently of a newborn.	SS: Sally with Kids L/3: Sally, Stay-at-Home Mother of 4

How difficult has it been for you to lose the weight? • I'm 35 lbs over from my second and can't seem to get back. • I eat all the things I give the kids Seem to have constant cravings	B-ROLL: Sally at home feeding herself and kids in frumpy T-shirt SALLY CROSSES TO STAGE
Scott, Can you help her? I work to eliminate cravings • Scott asks Sally—what is your worse craving • Short hypnotic process • Show acupressure points	CLOSE-UP HYPNOTIC PROCESS MUSIC FX
HOST to SALLY, What are you feeling as Scott is working with you?	
HOST RECAPS WITH SCOTT WHAT TECHNIQUES HE USED	FSCG: Information Hypnosis Process Acupressure Points to reduce cravings
ADD DISCLAIMER TO HOME VIEWER Obviously, to do this at home you would need a health care professionally trained.	
SALLY, How do you feel? Hopeful, I've tried everything else	
TEASE: Scott, We won't have time to see whether or not this has any lasting results. So we are going to invite you both back this Friday, and Scott, what will you bring with you on your return? Part of Sally's success will depend on	

exercise so I will bring the Vegas show-girls and we'll show her exercise techniques she can do at home while she's still being mom.	
SALLY, How's that sound? • Great	
OUTRO: Thank you Sally. Thank you Scott. You can check out Scott at Doctor Scott Lewis dot com. We'll be right back.	FSCG: www.DrScottLewis.com MUSIC: FX

The Talk-Down

Before you arrive, probably the night before, the producer does a *talk-down* with the director and the crew to talk about the technical execution of the show.

They literally talk down from A to Z what is expected to happen. Who goes where, etc. The director and the crew usually work off a modified version of the script called the *rundown*, which looks like following:

[*Segment #6*
Show Title: Millie Really Talk Show
Producer: Jacquie Jordan
Associate producer: Mark Parsons
TRT: 7:00
TD: 9/25/05   AD: 10/5/05

AUDIO: 3 lavs, 1 hand-held
GUEST: Scott Lewis, DC
AUDIENCE MEMBER: Sally Jennings
SEATING: 2 barstools downstage h/b

HOST INTRO	LIVE BUMP-IN SHOT B-ROLL: Vegas Show Girl Work Out video w/ Guest Helping Show Girls
Scott Lewis Entrance stage left	Close-Up L/3: Scott Lewis, D.C., Stage Hypnotist
Q&A	B-ROLL: Vegas Showgirls L/3: Vegas Showgirl Workout B-ROLL: Scott at his office with patients and Scott at night his show at Riviera.
HOST CROSSES TO AUDIENCE INTRO GUEST FRONT RT AISLE	GUEST: Sally Jennings PROP: Hand-held mike
Q&A	SS: Sally with Kids L/3: Sally, Stay-at-Home Mother of 4
GUEST CROSSES TO H/B w/ HOST—ALL 3 GUESTS STAND UP	
Q&A	Music FX
RECAP	FSCG: Information Hypnosis process Acupressure points to reduce cravings
DISCLAIMER	
TEASE	
OUTRO	FSCG: www.DrScottLewis.com LIVE BUMP-OUT SHOT MUSIC: FX FADE TO BLACK

During your briefing, the producer will talk you through the physical action that will take place. Oftentimes, a stage manager will get you from the green room and block you through the movement of the segment if your segment requires action other than you having been pre-set at home base.

As you can see, both documents are fairly straightforward. Most of us have read plays at some point in our education: scripts and rundowns are like close kissing cousins. There are stage directions and dialogue and that's about it. My only concern is that you focus on your performance and your performance alone. This book is meant to empower you with knowledge and encourage your performance and then the rest is up to us!

Wired for Sound

Like doctors, tailors, and ballroom dancing instructors, audio technicians are one of the few professional people we allow up close and personal. After the segment walk through, an audio technician will come to the green room and want to help you with your blouse, shirt, or jacket. Why are they so friendly?

The audio technician will be helping reposition your clothes: he or she will be attaching a small and unobtrusive *lavaliere* microphone to your person. And I was just kidding about up close and personal before. Audio technicians are consummate professionals and have attached thousands of lavalieres to scores of guests. You've probably seen these mikes before: sometimes they are visibly clipped to a man's tie, for instance, or the collar of a guest's T-shirt. They are perfect for picking up the sound of your voice and enable you to keep your hands free for gestures or demonstrations of your product. Throughout a show, hosts often switch between using hand-held mikes and lavalieres.

A word of caution: a lavaliere will be able to pick up your voice within a significant range through the set and backstage, so do be careful about what you say, as audio technicians and even the director can be listening on the same channel. They won't be spying on you of course; they are too busy for such activities. But a stray comment or joke might be overheard.

I once had a mischievous lavaliere-wired guest who tricked another backstage guest into an overly frank admission about one of the associate producers, who was deemed "so incredibly boring." The producer happened to be on the same channel and overheard this remark. Luckily, the producer was a good sport and saw the humor in the guest's little bit of verbal horseplay. But this tale illustrates an important point: everything you say when you are miked can be unintentionally eavesdropped upon. And I hate to make any of you uneasy, but that includes trips to the rest room. Whistling tunefully (or even off-key) might serve to obscure the natural background noises of a restroom trip, but just in case you are not an Olympic-level whistler, you can ask a production assistant or audio technician to have the mike turned off while you take that trip down the hall. Again, I'm only jesting slightly here! I want you to avoid embarrassment prior to stepping out on stage for that big moment.

Preparing for Your Big Moment

Now that your mike is attached you will be escorted to the set, where you will await your cue from the stage manager. You will be *quite nervous.* In fact, if a producer could, they would insist that you be nervous! Why? Because nervousness creates great camera energy.

I worry when a guest is casual about walking out in front of a studio audience and speaking in front of multiple cameras and banks of studio lights. Do they really care about making great TV? Do they just want to make their sales pitch and take the next plane back home? A lack of nervous anticipation almost always translates into a lack of energy. The way I see it, if you're not ready to throw up, then I'm off in a corner throwing up! If you aren't bussing, something is amiss.

So a case of nerves is entirely appropriate in any and all television appearances! Stomach butterflies are welcome, and, as you now know, a sought-after sensation from a producer's POV.

What to Do When You're Finally On Air

You have been escorted to the set. It is now officially way too late for any new ideas to be brought up. The show is in motion, as is your appearance. You might have just had a sudden, last-minute brainstorm as to how to improve your segment or product pitch, but alas, the time for improvising and revising is long past. Even if you realize that we had been misspelling your name all along and that the onscreen graphics that introduced you would all be wrong too, it is simply too late. That's because the stage manager has received word via radio from the director. He is giving you your cue to make your entrance...

> It's showtime!

There are many cameras on a TV set. Do not worry for a moment which one to look at, because that is the director's job. He is off in the control room looking at all the camera points of view at once. He calls out which camera shot he thinks is best and the technical director executes these instructions. They are dealing with the influx of visual information. All you have to do is walk out on stage, shake hands with the host, sit down in a chair, and be yourself.

While you are onstage, there is one rule to remember and act upon above all others: you are not being interviewed, you are *having a conversation* with the host and any other guests present. You do not need permission to speak. You do need to give yourself permission to participate.

When we converse normally, without the presence of an audience and cameras, we usually wait for eye contact or body language before we speak. But here on a television set you do *not* have to wait for this natural cue. Because you are on microphone at all times, the moment that you speak, the director will hear this in the control room and one of the cameras will find you. Another important rule to keep in mind: you do not need to wait to for the host's attention or "I'm listening to you" body language before you jump in and say what needs to be said. You've been walked through the segment by a producer. You know how the subject under discussion is supposed to unfold. You can follow the same pre-scripted plan of action and get into the game. You've come all this way to shine, baby, so don't be a polite dormouse! Be proactive. Be high energy. This is your segment, so *own it.*

Guess what? Sometimes hosts are not well prepared. Or they get tired and fuzzy and they lose focus. So sometimes a host will inadvertently stray from the pre-scripted beats. This means that the segment's direction will change, often not for the better. But remember this: the producer has briefed you and told you precisely what to expect. Heck, what you expect is what we expect too, but sometimes the hosts, well, they stray. Because you have been informed in advance what you will be getting out of the segment, *you need to take yourself there if the host moves off topic.* I'm sorry that I cannot help you, but this is your problem. You have all the information you need to get the agreed upon point (or pitch, or plug) across.

But please don't overstep your boundaries or, as they say, "overstay your welcome." You are, after all, a guest. And the host is the host, and you are invited to *their* party. There is nothing more uncomfortable for all parties involved, including the viewer, when a guest bullies their way through a segment. It ruins the party for everyone, and you can be assured never to be invited back. However, with that said, the worst thing a guest can say to me after a taping is "I didn't have a chance to say this...I didn't have a chance to say that... The host never asked me this...the time was too short...went too fast." I'm sorry, friend, if you're not empowered here to own your segment—like in a marriage, owning your part—I can't help you after the segment is over. Seize the moment.

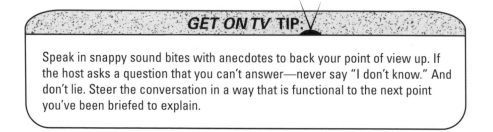

GET ON TV TIP:

Speak in snappy sound bites with anecdotes to back your point of view up. If the host asks a question that you can't answer—never say "I don't know." And don't lie. Steer the conversation in a way that is functional to the next point you've been briefed to explain.

But you know what? I know that you will be diligent about applying your *Get on TV* knowledge to your TV career, and I also know that you'll develop this knowledge into an active set of skills that will make you the kind of guest or expert that gets asked back by producers time and time again. Take the TV game seriously, and it will take you seriously.

Do's and Don'ts: Tips for a Successful Segment

DO: Energy is important, so *smile* as much as possible provided that the material is appropriate.

DON'T: Plug your book (or product or service) during the segment. You are on TV to provide information in a conversational manner. Do you prefer chatting to new people in social environments, or when they come knocking at your door without invitation? You need to sell yourself without pushing your book, etc. As a thank-you for appearing on a show, you will get a proper plug at the appropriate (and scripted!) point in the segment. Let the host plug you. Don't plug yourself.

DO: Prepare anecdotes that you can use to rein in a runway segment, or for when you may drift off topic.

DON'T: Throw off a conversation. Behave as you would as if you were in somebody else's house. If a host strays off topic, do not bulldoze your way back towards the scripted beats: be gracious! If for whatever reason another guest becomes unexpectedly confrontational, keep a cool head. Shouting may not show you off in the best light!

DO: Get your message out early and use examples to illustrate your point, product, etc. Time flies during a segment, so make sure you get your main point across!

DON'T: Give an answer or make a statement that you are unsure of. If you do find yourself saying something that you are not 100 percent about, qualify the statement—"Of course, I am not certain about that, but to the best of my knowledge it is true..." Never ever lie, because you'll get caught. Guests that lie will not get asked back and they may develop a bad reputation, or even get blackballed entirely.

DO: Make the host look good! You do this when you are prepared, engaged, and have high energy. If a host seems like they aren't getting you or your story or product, help them out by steering the segments back on topic.

I recently saw a train wreck moment on TV where a host asked a generic question trying to get into the conversation and the guest dropped the ball. It went like this:

HOST: You've been recovered from multiple sclerosis for seven years.

GUEST: Oh no, not that long. <done with answer>

Ouch! Albeit, it was a terrible lead question, but where was the guest in that moment? A proper response would have been, "I've been recovered for an amazing five years and am eager to tell you how I came to that recovery."

This would have lead the host back into the next question and the purpose of the interview.

Chapter 11

Getting Real on Reality TV

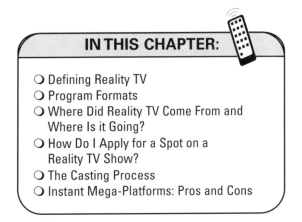

IN THIS CHAPTER:

- Defining Reality TV
- Program Formats
- Where Did Reality TV Come From and Where Is it Going?
- How Do I Apply for a Spot on a Reality TV Show?
- The Casting Process
- Instant Mega-Platforms: Pros and Cons

Defining Reality TV

If you don't already know about reality TV, you may have been locked in a fallout shelter for the past ten years, or were perhaps napping alongside Rip Van Winkle under a willow tree. But as this is a how-to book, let's be formal and thorough and define our terms. Reality television is a genre of programming that portrays real people in a variety of situations. In other words, there are no actors and no pre-scripted storylines.

GENRE

A type or category of television programming.

Reality TV has taken off like a rocket since the advent of *Survivor* and the prime-time game show *Who Wants to be a Millionaire?* Networks and studios love reality programming because, when compared to the cost of a sitcom or one-hour drama, they are dirt cheap. There are no writers to pay and no actors to hire and pay *residuals* to.

RESIDUALS

A payment made to a performer, writer, or director for each repeat showing of a recorded television show or commercial.

And the lower cost of a production means higher profit from advertising revenue. Remember when the cast of *Friends* renegotiated for hefty multimillion-dollar paydays in that show's final season? If you are producing a reality TV show, even a massively successful one, there are no stars to make salary demands.

Also, dramas and sitcoms only become significantly profitable when they can be *syndicated* and resold to local markets, which then broadcast reruns at any time of the day or night. And to sell a syndication package of shows, there has to be at least one hundred episodes in the can. At twenty-two episodes per year, that's a five-year commitment before the cash comes rolling in. Networks and producers that create and finance reality TV producers don't have to worry about getting to that magic one hundredth episode: their shows are so low cost that advertising revenues can offer an "instant" return on their investment. For the shows that are successful, reality TV is a "pay as you go" investment. And failures are low cost, especially when compared to expensive sitcom and drama flops, in which a star's contract may stipulate full payment for episodes that never get made.

So, seen in this light, a reality TV show is like a big party you might organize in your back yard, complete with games and activities. A sitcom or drama equates with a back yard play in which you'll have to invest in a stage, a script, actors, costumes, props, lights, backstage crew, the whole ball of wax. Can you see the appeal in terms of capital investment? Reality TV is fast and fun and you won't loose your shirt if a show fails.

So that's *what* reality TV is, but why has it become popular? The jury's out on that one, but there are several possible reasons. The first is that the quality of network sitcoms and dramas has declined, thus making reality TV a blast of fresh air in a stale environment. Why has this decline in our beloved shows happened? Partly due to cable TV, which, as a subscriber service, can afford to pick and choose what it makes. Award winning shows like *The Sopranos* or *Six Feet Under* are where much of the "action" is as far as originality goes. Part of this decline is due to the aforementioned expense of making sitcoms and dramas. Networks tend to be very cautious as to what they think an audience will like in terms of new programming, so they tend to stick to the same old formulas. When one show hits, the next season there is almost always several imitations, usually ones that fade from view with great rapidity. While the "familiarity factor" can work to a network's advantage, as is the case with the runaway successes of the *CSI* and *Law and Order* franchises, overall, audiences have tired of the same old same old. So when *Survivor* hit the airwaves, it found a huge audience of parched and thirsty viewers ready to drink in the new.

Program Formats

There are three basic reality TV programming formats. There is the *documentary* program, in which a person or a group of people have their every moment taped by a camera crew. The camera's POV is that of a "fly on the wall," observing but never interfering with the action. MTV's *Real World,* produced by pioneering production company Bunim/Murray Productions, is the most famous example of this format of reality television programming, which can be viewed as *documentary soap operas* because most of the conflict arises from personal squabbles, personality conflicts and the inevitable love affairs. The format has taken another evolutionary step in recent years by focusing on celebrities: *The Osbournes* was an international smash, and even Anna Nicole Smith and Jessica Simpson have enough fame to garner their own shows.

Next came an interesting fusion between the documentary and game show genres, in which cameras followed people or groups of people as they set about completing a series of tasks. This programming format is fluid. A show such as *Fear Factor* plays out like a modern take on an old-school game show, only far more edgy. *Survivor* follows the same general path, but there is much more focus on the day-to-day activities of the show's contestants. This general category continues to throw out new twists. Shows like *The Bachelor* and *The Apprentice* have a more focused goal than *Survivor*. These shows pitch their prizes in their high concept titles, but they are still following the game show/documentary soap paradigm.

The *talent search show* is another offshoot of the basic game show/documentary soap format. *American Idol* is the most famous and successful talent show. Like the syndicated series *Star Search, Idol* uses a twist to the standard format of a talent show, in which contestants are evaluated solely by a panel of judges. The twist is audience participation: both shows utilize the opinion of the studio audience as co-judges. *American Idol* ups the ante and takes the concept one step further by involving the show's entire broadcast audience to vote in the final phases of the competition.

HIGH CONCEPT

Designed to appeal to a mass audience by incorporating popular, glamorous features.

Another reality programming format is comparatively rare and is best represented by MTV's half-hour program *Punk'd* (translation for the elderly: "punked" means "fooled" or "made a fool of"). These shows use hidden cameras to observe unsuspecting individuals as they deal with carefully staged scenarios designed to become more and more outlandish, obnoxious, or slapstick the longer they last. While intended mainly for comic purposes, the show often reveals much about human nature, and how we all deal with certain social situations. *Punk'd* usually tries to provoke their target's egos, as the show exclusively plays its pranks on unsuspecting celebrities. *Punk'd* is a direct descendant of *Candid Camera*, which first debuted in 1953. The long-running show was the brainchild of Allan Funt, who can be considered one of the founding fathers of what has become known as reality television. *Candid Camera* observed regular everyday folks instead of celebrities, which made its comic moments all the more universal.

Where Did Reality TV Come From and Where Is It Going?

Reality TV...where did it all begin? That's open to a variety of interpretations. Perhaps the modern day format's roots lie in documentary film-making and radio/TV "man on the street" interviews, in which regular folks were asked for their opinions on a particular subject. We like to see how others live as well as hear what they have to say. Are they the same as we are? If not, how are they different? Although most reality TV programming is entirely entertainment-oriented, its root appeal lies in our endless fascination with other people, because understanding or even just observing their lives gives us perspective on our own.

Remember the motion picture *The Truman Show*, from 1998? In it, Jim Carrey played a man who had unwittingly been the focus of a documentary TV program since his birth. The movie anticipated our fascination with the "new wave" of reality TV that was yet to materialize.

The year 1992 saw the arrival of MTV's long-running series *The Real World*, created by pioneering producers the late Mary-Ellis Bunim and Jonathan Murray. Each season follows seven strangers who live in a house together and are taped almost continually. The massive amount of taped material is then cleverly edited down into half-hour shows that have the dramatic structure of a soap opera episode, complete with ongoing subplots and cliffhanger endings.

Soon after *Survivor* burst onto the national stage with gigantic ratings, there was much media speculation that the reality TV boom was a fad that would run its course then go bust. But these doomsayers have been proven wrong. Reality television looks as if it is has become a permanent fixture of our complex and colorful popular culture.

What direction will reality programming take next? Well if you know, you're going to make a bundle, because everybody is looking for the next big thing, the next new wave. How about "Spy TV," a candid camera variant played seriously, in which two separate people's lives are secretly videotaped and they are manipulated into a non-threatening conflict by actors playing various roles? What about a Mr. Deeds program that follows a politician to Washington, DC? Anybody for *Who Wants to Be a Librarian*? Or what about a historical-conspiratorial scavenger hunt show modeled on *The Da Vinci Code*? No idea is too small or too large, save perhaps for *Survivor on the Moon*, and even that show will no doubt get an airdate when we get around to building domed lunar cities!

Most likely, the next wave will be unexpected, and will sound totally fresh. Even TV producers have to retool their pitches with new hooks.

How Do I Apply for a Spot on a Reality TV Show?

How do you become a contestant on a reality TV show? Simple: fill out an application, just like a job interview. If you Google (or Yahoo or use whatever search engine you are partial to) the words *Survivor* and application, you'll find a link to an official CBS website where you can download an application. The same will hold true for most of the established shows that plan a new season. Because this is television, you will have to submit a video of yourself, in which will almost certainly be expected to pitch yourself to the producers. You'll have a few minutes to explain who you are and why you would make an ideal candidate for the show in question. The 2004 *Survivor* show had an iron-clad rule: any video longer than three minutes would not be considered. Your lessons in crafting hooks, pitching yourself, and show reel construction and presentation will come in handy here. Make your audition tape count and make it good. I expect no less from you now that you are all set to begin your television careers! Make me proud!

Of course, there are always new shows each and every season. Where do these candidates come from? Do they have an inside line? Well, yes and no. They are simply people who have seen new show casting calls in their local newspapers. Most of them probably found out about the hypothetical new show by chance. But you can bet that a significant number of applicants were already highly motivated to find such opportunities. It's all a matter of keeping your eyes open. There are numerous websites devoted to reality television that post casting calls and open application submissions, such as www.realitytvworld.com and www.beonrealitytv.com. I do not officially endorse either site (although they both look very fine to me), so keep searching until you narrow down your own preferred choices as to Internet resources. (Warning: this kind of show information is free to anybody. If any site or other business tries to charge you for the privilege of being on their email list or other subscriber services, look elsewhere.) *Variety* and *The Hollywood Reporter* will also post information about new shows, although you'll either have to subscribe or make multiple visits to your local library to keep yourself up to speed. The best bet to stay informed is via the Internet, where you will also be able to locate chat groups that share information and opinions about reality TV shows.

CHAT GROUP

A set of people who communicate regularly via the Internet, either in real time or by email, about a particular topic.

One last tip: a great indicator of a professionally run reality TV website is the frequency of its new postings. If a site has posted no fresh information (even trivial tidbits) for more than a week or two, keep looking. Silence, in this case, is certainly not golden.

The Casting Process

Now bear in mind that show policies will vary: what follows is a rule of thumb guide that will help you know what, in general, to expect.

If your application is accepted by the show you've sent your materials to, you will most likely have to travel to NYC or L.A. at your own expense for an interview. If you make it through the interview phase, the show's production company will then pay to fly you out for the final selection process. If you do get cast, you are going to have to sign a contract with the production company and studio that places certain strict limitations on you *and* your family. This is because most reality shows rely on surprise twists that can get spoiled if anybody spills the beans prior to a show's airtime. There may be moratoriums on when you can accept a booking on TV or radio. Some shows may want you to give interviews to their network affiliates first, then other network's outlets. If you want to play ball, you have to play by the rules.

Sasha Alpert, a Los Angeles–based vice president of casting who casts for the reality production company Bunim-Murray, says that in the end an audition reel should convey "charismatic storytellers with good energy." Many of Sasha's castings have catapulted many television careers—Kyle Brandt and Melissa Howard were each on *The Real World–Chicago,* and now Kyle appears on *Days of Our Lives,* while Melissa is on *Girls Behaving Badly.*

Putting together an audition reel for a reality show should involve the same techniques as discussed in the book. 1) Make sure your hook matches the show you are appearing on, 2) Your tape should be like your movie trailer, and 3) it should capture your essence.

Instant Mega-Platforms: Pros and Cons

The major benefit of being on a reality TV show as it relates to our purposes is this: you instantly have a ready-made, nationwide, celebrity platform upon which to launch your career as a TV guest or expert. That's on the pro side, and it's a *huge* factor to have on your side.

What's the con side of the equation? Well, the first thing is this: you have to have something to sell beyond being a former contestant on *Reality Show X.* You will get booked because you were a contestant especially if you did or were part of a memorable moment on the show. But the media cycle spins quickly, and unless you're one of the finalists or winners, your moment in the sun vis-à-vis your show-related bookings will quickly fade.

Another con factor is not having something to sell or say beyond reflecting on your recent experience. *Survivor: The Australian Outback* contestant Elisabeth Hasselbeck parlayed her initial bookings into a co-host spot on *The View.* But she did not just luck into this position: she had a goal in mind (being a television presenter) and she had the talent to capitalize on a major opportunity when it arose.

The flip side is that reality shows offer an entire new landscape of guest appearance opportunities. Dr. Reef Karim, a faculty psychiatrist at UCLA, has an entirely separate career as a notable television guest appearing on reality shows including *Extreme Makeover* and VH-1's *Love Lounge.*

For a budding or even a well-established TV guestpert, this chapter is about keeping your eye on the big horizon, reality television—which exemplifies the growth of opportunities that come out of being on TV. As you stay focused on building your hooks, pitches, and platforms, know that reality TV is looking for its next Clay Aiken in all the genres. From there, these folks use the same methods as described in this book to take their careers to the next level, and so can you.

Epilogue

There is nothing like the high from nailing an on-air performance when you know that there was a great exchange of energy, excitement, enthusiasm, and information with the host. Walking off the set is a most unbelievable feeling. And if you think it felt good, know that it appeared even stronger. Congratulations! The hard work, patience, and perseverance paid off.

I believe the experience of being on TV is much like writing and mailing a letter. The performance itself is like writing a letter. It's a form of expression and you are in the moment. When you watch yourself on TV later, it's like the experience of reading a letter that you sent to yourself in the mail. Believe it or not, they are two fundamentally different experiences. And I would bet that nine out of ten times you did better than you think, if you truly have done your work along the way. But nothing can prepare you for watching yourself on TV. And it often feels different seeing yourself than it felt while you were performing. With time and practice, both of those feelings should match up—and you will see what you feel…confident! But in the beginning, it does feel awkward watching yourself.

Where do you go from here? Well, you've worked really hard to get that producer's attention. By all means, follow up. From experience, I can say that most TV guestperts don't follow up. I think that's kind of ironic given how long it's taken them to bang on the doors to get in. A simple email (I prefer a handwritten note or even a postcard) is a simple way to stay in touch. This is the relationship that you now want to continue to foster from show to show. You want to be on the producer's go-to list when he or she needs ideas or referrals.

Many long-term television careers have been born out of being a TV guestpert. No matter what brought you here or what you've decided you need to get out of it…know that we, the TV producers, are looking for you! And now you have all the tools you need to get on TV!

Jacquie Jordan

Television and Cable Networks from A to Z

A&E
Arts and Entertainment
235 E. 45th St.
New York, NY 10017
Office: (212) 210-1340
Fax: (212) 850-9304
www.ae.com

ABC
One of the three original major networks

New York Office:
7 West 66th Street, 9th Floor
New York, NY 10023
(212) 456-7777

California Office:
500 S. Buena Vista St.
Burbank, CA 91521
(818) 460-7477
www.abc.com

ABC Family
Features family-oriented series and original programming
10960 Wilshire Blvd.
Los Angeles, CA 90024
(212) 456-7777
www.abcfamilychannel.com

ABC News
Features national/worldwide news
7 West 66th Street
New York, NY 10023
(212) 456-7777

Altitude Sports and Entertainment
Features the Nuggets, Avalanche, Mammoth, and minor league, college, and high school sports. Provides the Rocky Mountain region with sports programs, including outdoor and lifestyle shows and entertainment programs.
1000 Chopper Circle
Denver, CO 80204
(303) 405-1100
www.altitude.tv

AMC
The premier 24-hour movie network featuring award-winning original productions about the world of American film. It has one of the finest, most comprehensive libraries of classic films and a diverse blend of original series and documentaries. And it is home to my favorite show, *Sunday Morning Shootout,* hosted by Hollywood icon Peter Guber and editor-in-chief of *Variety* Peter Bart.
200 Jericho Quadrangle
Jericho, NY 11753
(516) 396-3000
www.amctv.com

The America Channel
Programs about America, its people, and the American experience.
120 International Parkway, Suite 220
Heathrow, FL 32746
(407) 333-3031
www.americachannel.us

America One Network
The "voice of the homeland."
6125 Airport Freeway, Ste. 100
Haltom City, TX 76117
(817) 546-1400
www.americaone.com

American Life TV Network
The baby boomer network.
650 Massachusetts Avenue
Washington, DC 20001
(202) 289-6633
www.goodtv.com

Animal Planet
Brings viewers face-to-face with creatures from around the globe. Features visits to people and their pets, plus lively nature shows tailored especially for children.
7700 Wisconsin Avenue
Bethesda, MD 20814
(301) 986-1999
www.animal.discovery.com

BBC America
British television brought to viewers in the United States.
7475 Wisconsin Avenue, Ste.1100
Bethesda, MD 20814
(301) 347-2222
www.bbcamerica.com

Black Entertainment Television (BET)
BET, Inc., a subsidiary of Viacom, Inc., is the leading African American multimedia entertainment company.
1900 W. Place
Washington, DC 20018
(202) 608-2800
www.bet.com

BET Action PPV
Features urban-oriented movies from all the major studios as well as independent studio fare; will also offer event programming, which could include gospel music.
1900 W. Place, NE
Suite #800
Los Angeles, CA 90067
support@bet.com

The Biography Channel
This network from A&E offers movies, documentaries, and short features profiling historic figures, entertainers, and other notable individuals.
235 E. 45th St.
New York, NY 10017
(212) 210-1340
www.biographychannel.com

Black Belt TV
Martial arts programming consisting of movies, sports, and news.
P.O. Box 3215
San Dimas, CA 91773
(909) 971-9300
www.blackbelttv.com

Black Entertainment Television Movies (BET Movies)
Features BET, Inc. movies.
1235 W Street
Washington, DC 20018
(202) 608-2230
www.bet.com

BloombergTV

24-hour coverage of financial news and markets from reporters who add perspective and analysis.
499 Park Avenue
New York, NY 10022
(212) 318-2000
www.bloomberg.com/tv

BNN

Boston Neighborhood Network (BNN) is operated by the Boston Community Access and Programming Foundation. Established by Boston's cable franchise agreement in 1983, BNN's primary goals are to serve the city of Boston and expand the constitutional rights of freedom of expression for all people. Through the Boston Charitable Trust, major funding for BNN is from cable television subscribers in Boston.
8 Park Plaza
Suite 2240
Boston, MA 02116
Offices: (617) 720-2113
Fax: (617) 720-3781
www.bnntv.org

Bravo

Film and arts network.
2 Park Ave, 11th Floor
New York, NY 10016
(212) 561-3303
www.bravotv.com

Buena Vista Television

Create and distribute various television programs attached to Disney.
500 S. Buena Vista
Burbank, CA 91521
(818) 560-1000
www.bvtv.com
bvtv.researchsupport@disney.com

Cartoon Network

Network broadcasting animated entertainment geared towards children.
1050 Techwood Drive NW
Atlanta, GA 30318
www.cartoonnetwork.com

CBS

One of the major networks.
51 West 52nd Street
New York, NY
(212) 975-3247
www.cbs.com

CBS News
One of the major news networks.
524 West 57th St.
New York, NY 10019
(212) 975-3247
www.cbsnews.com

Channel One
A learning community of 12,000 American middle, junior, and high schools representing
over 8 million students and 400,000 educators.
6203 B. Variel Avenue
Woodland Hills, CA 91367
(818) 226-6200
(800) 805-5131
info@channelonetv.com
feedback@channelonetv.com

Christian Broadcast Network
Founded in 1960 by religious broadcaster Pat Robertson. Produces *NewsWatch Today* and
The 700 Club.
977 Centerville Turnpike
Virginia Beach, VA 23463
(757) 226-7000
www.cbn.org

The Church Channel
A TBN network that primarily features church services from a wide variety of denomina-
tions, including Protestant, Catholic, and Jewish faith groups.
2442 Michelle
Tustin, CA 92780
(714) 832-2950
www.churchchannel.org

Cine Latino
Mexican network.
Boulevard Puerto Aéreo 486
Col. Moctezuma
Mexico D.F.
+52 (0)55 5764 8211

Cinemax
Pay movie channel.
1100 Avenue of the Americas
New York, NY 10036
(212) 512-1000
www.cinemax.com

Classic Sports Network/ESPN Classics
Classic Sports Network was bought by ESPN.
ESPN Plaza
Bristol, CT 06010
http://sports.espn.go.com/sitetools/s/contact/classicsport.html

CMT
Country music videos and programming.
2806 Opryland Drive
Nashville, TN 37214
(615) 335-8350
www.cmt.com

CNBC
Financial news highlights dominate the day, while nights include features and discussions of contemporary business issues.
900 Sylvan Ave
Englewood Cliffs, NJ 07632
(877) 251-5685
http://moneycentral.msn.com/cnbc/tv/

C-NET Network
CNET Channel is a subsidiary of CNET Networks (NASDAQ: CNET), a premier global interactive content company that informs, entertains, and connects large, engaged audiences around topics of high information need or personal passion.
235 Second Street
San Francisco, CA 94105
(415) 344-2000
www.cnetnetworks.com

CNN
The fastest, most complete 24-hour coverage of breaking news. CNN offers programs ranging from business to sports to entertainment, as well as topical interviews and *Larry King Live*.
One CNN Center
Box 105366
Atlanta, GA 33048
(404) 827-1700
www.cnn.com

CNNfn
CNNfn delivers twelve hours of comprehensive business and stock market news from 7 a.m. to 7 p.m. ET daily.
5 Penn Plaza
20th Floor
New York, NY 10001
(212) 714-7800
http://cnnfn.cnn.com

CNN Headline News
One CNN Center
Atlanta, GA 30348-5366
www.cnn.com/HLN/
headline.news@cnn.com

Comcast Sports Net (West, Mid-Atlantic, Chicago)
A new 24-hour, 7-day-a-week sports and entertainment television network.
Comcast SportsNet
7700 Wisconsin Avenue, Suite 200
Bethesda, MD 20814
(301) 718-3200
www.comcastsportsnet.com

Comedy Central
Original programming and movies with a comedic theme.
1775 Broadway
New York, NY 10019
(212) 767-8600
www.comedycentral.com

Court TV
Focuses on current law cases and trials.
600 3rd Avenue
New York, NY 10016
(800) COURT 56
www.courttv.com

CSPAN 1, 2, 3
Networks dedicated to different news forums and government processes.
400 North Capitol Street NW
Ste. 650
Washington, DC 20001
(202) 737-3220
www.c-span.org

CSTV: College Sport Television
A new 24-hour network dedicated to the best in college sports. Programming features in-depth, original news and information and exclusive games and championships of over 25 men's and women's sports from almost every major conference.
Chelsea Piers, Pier 62
New York, NY 10011
(212) 342-8700
www.collegesports.com

DayStar Television Network

The fastest-growing Christian network in America. Interdenominational and multicultural, Daystar features the nation's leading ministries. More live remote broadcasts of major Christian events than any other network.
P.O. Box 612066
Dallas, TX 75261-2066
www.daystar.com

Discovery

Offers real-life nonfiction entertainment covering nature, science and technology, history, and world exploration.
7700 Wisconsin Avenue
Bethesda, MD 20814
(301) 986-1999
http://dsc.discovery.com

Discovery Español

Discovery in Spanish.
1 Discovery Place
Silver Spring, MD 20910
(240) 662-0000
http://tudiscovery.com

Discovery Health

Health news and in-depth features, show information, and health library.
7700 Wisconsin Avenue
Bethesda, MD 20814
(301) 986-1999
http://dsc.discovery.com

Discovery Home

Offers expert advice and creative ideas that inspire us to improve our homes, our surroundings, and the way we live.
7700 Wisconsin Avenue
Bethesda, MD 20814
(301) 986-1999
viewer_relations@discovery.com

Discovery Kids

Enables kids to learn about and develop a variety of adventures and explorations.
7700 Wisconsin Avenue
Bethesda, MD 20814
(301) 986-1999
http://dsc.discovery.com

Discovery Times

Offers today's news, Discovery style.
1 Discovery Place
Silver Spring, MD 20910
(240) 662-0000
http://times.discovery.com

Discovery Wings
Offers various programs about military topics.
1 Discovery Place
Silver Spring, MD 20910
(240) 662-0000
http://wings.discovery.com

Disney Channel
Original programming and replayed Disney products geared to a young audience.
3800 West Alameda Avenue
Burbank, CA 91505
(818) 569-7500
www.disney.com/DisneyChannel

Do-It-Yourself
The do-it-yourself network.
9721 Sherrill Blvd.
Knoxville, TN 37932
(865) 694-2700
www.diynetwork.com

E! Entertainment Television
Programming based on entertainment, style, and celebrities.
5750 Wilshire Blvd.
Los Angeles, CA 90036
(323) 692-4815
www.eonline.com

Encore
Pay movie channel.
8900 Liberty Circle
Englewood, CO 80112
(720) 852-7700
http://encore.encoremedia.com

Encore Westerns
Movie channel focusing on the western genre.
8900 Liberty Circle
Englewood, CO 80112
(720) 852-7700
http://westerns.encoremedia.com

Endemol USA
Production company specifically producing reality TV.
9255 Sunset Blvd., Ste. 1100
Los Angeles, CA 90069
(310) 860-9914
www.endemol.com

ESPN
Network broadcasting sporting events and original programming.
ESPN Plaza
935 Middle St.
Bristol, CT 06010
(860) 766-2000
www.espn.com

ESPN 2
Network broadcasting sporting events and original programming.
ESPN Plaza
935 Middle St.
Bristol, CT 06010
(860) 766-2000
www.espn.com

ESPN Classic
Sports network that shows events from the past.
ESPN Plaza
935 Middle St.
Bristol, CT 06010
(860) 766-2000
www.espn.com

ESPN News
24 hours a day news about sports.
ESPN Plaza
935 Middle St.
Bristol, CT 06010
(860) 766-2000
www.espn.com

EWTN
Watch live Papal events, masses, documentaries, dramas and teaching series, plus children's animation from producers throughout Latin America and the world.
www.ewtn.com

Fine Living Channel
Dedicated to the pursuit of personal passions and the art of getting the most from every moment in life.
5757 Wilshire Blvd.
Los Angeles, CA 90036
www.fineliving.com

First TV
P.O. Box 332
Wyoming, IL 61491

FitTV
The only network delivering quality programming to men, women, and families who are interested in enhancing their well-being through exercise, personal trainers, and motivational advice.
7700 Wisconsin Avenue
Bethesda, MD 20814
(301) 986-1999
www.fit.discovery.com

FLIX
Movie Network
1633 Broadway
New York, NY 10019
(800) 422-9000

The Food Network
Original programming based on food and cooking.
1177 Avenue of the Americas
New York, NY 10036
(212) 398-8836
www.foodtv.com

FOX
One of the major networks.
2121 Avenue of the Stars
Los Angeles, CA 90067
(310) 369 2000
www.fox.com

FOX Movie Channel
Cable channel showing Fox movies.
P.O. Box 900
Beverly Hills, CA 90213
www.thefoxmoviechannel.com

FOX News
Around-the-clock news coverage.
1211 Avenue of the Americas
New York, NY 10036
(888) 369-4762
www.foxnews.com

FOX Reality
Under development.
2121 Avenue of the Stars
Los Angeles, CA 90067
(310) 369-2000
www.foxreality.com

FOX Sports Net
Sports network that focuses on specific regions of the country.
10201 W. Pico Blvd., Bldg. 101
Los Angeles, CA 90035
(310) 369 1000
www.foxsports.com

FOX Sports World
"The Greatest Soccer Network on Earth." This 24-hour channel is your passport to world-class soccer, championship rugby, and international sports news. Featured programming includes English Premier League Soccer and the Fox Sports World Report.
10201 W. Pico Blvd., Bldg. 101
Los Angeles, CA 90035
(310) 369-1000
www.foxsports.com/fsw

FOX Sports World Español
"The Greatest Soccer Network on Earth." This 24-hour channel is your passport to world-class soccer, championship rugby and international sports news. Featured programming includes English Premier League Soccer and the *Fox Sports World Report*.
10000 Santa Monica Blvd. Suite 333
Los Angeles, CA 90067
(310) 286-3800/ 286-3854

Fuel
A 24-hour cable network dedicated to the world of extreme sports.
www.fuel.tv

Fuse TV
Cable music video station.
1111 Stewart Ave.
Bethpage, NY 11714
www.fuse.tv

FX Networks
Network featuring original series and movies.
10000 Santa Monica Blvd.
Los Angeles, CA 90067
(310) 286-3800
www.fxnetworks.com

G4 Tech TV
Network focusing on video games and the people who play them.
12312 W. Olympic Blvd.
Los Angeles, CA 90064
(310) 979-5100
www.g4techtv.com

Galavision
Spanish language programming.
9405 NW 41st. St.
Miami, FL 33178
(305) 471-3900
www.galavision.com

Golf Channel
Offering event coverage, tips to help viewers with their golf game, and information about the most current equipment.
7580 Commerce Center Drive
Orlando, FL 32819
(407) 363-4653
www.thegolfchannel.com

Great American Country (GAC)
Home of the *Grand Ole Opry*. Gives country fans the best in country music videos as well as specials starring favorite country artists.
9697 East Mineral Avenue
Englewood, CO 80112
(303) 792-3111
www.gactv.com

GSN
Formerly know as the Game Show Network, features original game show programming along with older game show reruns.
10202 W. Washington Blvd.
Culver City, CA 90232
(310) 244-2222
www.gsn.com

Hallmark Channel
An entertainment network offering a diverse mix of family-friendly programming, the Hallmark Channel features original movies, television events, series, dramas, comedies, and real-life programs that combine strong storytelling with high quality production value.
12700 Ventura Blvd., Ste. 200
Studio City, CA 91604
(888) 390-7474
www.hallmarkchannel.com

HBO
Home Box Office, featuring various movies and original series.
2049 Century Park East, Suite 3600
Los Angeles, CA 90067
(310) 201-9200
www.hbo.com

HBO Family
Commercial-free programming suitable for children of all ages.
2049 Century Park East, Suite 3600
Los Angeles, CA 90067
(310) 201-9200
www.hbofamily.com

HBO Signature
Programming that appeals to today's smart, sassy, and sophisticated women.
2049 Century Park East, Suite 3600
Los Angeles, CA 90067
(310) 201-9200
www.hbo.com/hbosignature

HDNet
All high-definition national television network.
2400 N. Ulster St.
Denver, CO 80238
(303) 542-5600
www.hd.net

Headline News
Every 30 minutes, Turner Broadcasting's 24-hour news service delivers an updated, concise report on the day's top stories in business, sports, and entertainment news for the on-the-go viewer.
One CNN Center
Box 105366
Atlanta, GA 33048
(404) 827-1700
www.cnn.com

HGTV
The home and gardening channel
P.O. Box 50970
Knoxville, TN 37950
(423) 694-2700
www.hgtv.com

History Channel
Programming based on the study of history.
235 E. 45th St.
New York, NY 10017
(212) 210-1340
www.historychannel.com

Home Shopping Network

An interactive home shopping service offering a brand-name merchandise that consumers can purchase in the comfort of their homes.
1 HSN Drive
St. Petersburg, FL 33729
www.hsn.com

IFC

Independent film channel.
15 Crossways Park West
Woodbury, NY 11797
(516) 364-2222
www.ifctv.com

INHD

Digital cable network offers two channels of high-definition TV programming, including sports, movies, and music events.
www.inhd.com

Jewelry Television

Satellite-based network offering collectibles and jewelry. Offers online auctions, chat, and company store.
(865) 692-6100
www.jewelrytelevision.com

Jewish TV

Networked geared toward those of the Jewish faith.
13743 Ventura Blvd., Ste. 200
Sherman Oaks, CA 91423
(818) 789-5891
www.jewishtvnetwork.com

LATV

Latino music and entertainment, featuring original bilingual programming.
2323 Corinth Ave.
Los Angeles, CA 90064
(310) 943-LATV
www.latv.com

The Learning Channel (TLC)

Entertaining and informative family programming, including six commercial-free hours of weekday programming for preschoolers.
7700 Wisconsin Ave.
Bethesda, MD 20814
(888) 404-5969
www.tlc.discovery.com

Lifetime
Programming for women.
World Wide Plaza
309 West 49th St.
New York, NY 10019
www.lifetimetv.com

LOGO Channel
Cable channel providing programming for lesbian, gay, bisexual, and transgender adults.
1775 Broadway
11th floor
NY, NY 10019
www.logo-tv.com

Major Broadcasting Cable (MBC)
Programming for urban and African American communities.
800 Forrest St. NW
Atlanta, GA 30318
(404) 350-2509
www.mbcnetwork.com

MSNBC
News and financial programming.
1 MSNBC Plaza
Secaucus, NJ 07024
(888) MSNBC USA (676-2287)
www.msnbc.com

MTV
Music video television along with original programming.
1515 Broadway
New York, NY 10036
(212) 258-6000
www.mtv.com

MTV2
24-hour-a-day music videos.
1515 Broadway
New York, NY 10036
(212) 258-6000
www.mtv2.com

National Geographic Channel
Programming based on the *National Geographic* magazine.
1145 17th St. NW
Washington, DC 20036
(202) 912-6500
www.nationalgeographic.com/channel

NBA TV
NBA TV gives an insider's perspective on all the NBA action—in-depth game coverage and highlights, real-time stats and scores, NBA news, behind the scenes, plus great games from years past.
www.nba.com

NBC
One of the major national networks.
30 Rockefeller Plaza
Room 1802
New York, NY 10112
(212) 664-6046
www.nbc.com

NBC News
One of the major national news networks.
30 Rockefeller Plaza
New York, N.Y. 10112
www.nbcnews.com

NFL Network
NFL Network is a 24-hour, 7-day-a-week television network dedicated solely to the NFL during the season and throughout the off-season.
www.nfl.com

Nickelodeon
Programming for children and teens.
1515 Broadway
New York, NY 10036
(212) 258-7500
www.nick.com

The Outdoor Channel
Programming for the outdoor sportsman.
43445 Business Park Dr., Ste. 103
Temecula, CA 92590
(909) 699-6991
www.outdoorchannel.com

Oxygen
Programming for women, attempting to create a new kind of relationship between women and the media, based on honesty, humor, and heart.
75 Ninth Ave.
New York, NY 10011
(212) 651-2000
(323) 860-3500
www.oxygen.com

PAX

Family-oriented programming.
601 Clearwater Park Rd.
West Palm Beach, Florida 33401
(561) 682-4267
www.paxtv.com

PBS

Public Broadcasting Service.
1320 Braddock Place
Alexandria, VA 22314
(703) 739-5000
www.pbs.com

Playboy TV

Offers adult movies and original series.
2706 Media Center Dr.
Los Angeles, CA 90065
(323) 276-4000
www.playboy.com/playboytv

QVC

A home shopping network.
1365 Enterprise Drive
West Chester, PA 19380
(610) 701-1000
www.qvc.com

Rainbow Sport Network

On-demand sports and fitness instructional programming featuring Mia Hamm, Anna Kournikova, Bode Miller, Sue Bird, and other renowned sports authorities.
Rainbow Sports Networks Corporate
200 Jericho Quadrangle
Jericho, NY 11753

Reality TV USA

Reality programming 24 hours a day.
240 Center St.
El Segundo, CA 90266
(310) 356-4843
www.realitytvusa.com

RTN

The racetrack television network.
4175 Cameron Street
Suite B-10
Las Vegas, NV 89103
(866) 273-3726
www.rtn.tv

The Science Channel
Lets curious minds explore life's greatest mysteries and smallest wonders.
7700 Wisconsin Avenue
Bethesda, MD 20814
(301) 986-1999
http://dsc.discovery.com

Sci-Fi Channel
Programming geared toward the science fiction genre.
1230 Avenue of the Americas
New York, NY 10020
(212) 408-9100
www.scifi.com

Showtime
TV network featuring original series programming, cable movies, and current Hollywood hits.
1633 Broadway
New York, NY 10019
(212) 708-7302
www.sho.com

SoapNet
Network devoted to soaps and soap fans.
3800 W. Alameda Ave.
Burbank, CA 91505
(818) 569-3333
http://soapnet.go.com

Speed Channel
24-hour cable network devoted exclusively to automotive, aviation, and marine entertainment and information.
9711 Southern Pine Blvd.
Charlotte, NC 28273
(704) 731-2222
www.speedtv.com

Spike TV
Programming for men.
1515 Broadway
New York, NY 10036
(212) 846-4095
www.spiketv.com

Starz
Movie channel.
8900 Liberty Circle
Englewood, CO 80112
(720) 852 7700
http://starz.encoremedia.com

Style Network
24-hour network devoted to fashion, beauty, home, and entertaining.
5670 Wilshire Blvd.
Los Angeles, CA 90036
(323) 954-2400
www.stylenetwork.com

Sundance
Broadcasting movies that have been Sundance Film Festival selections and coverage of the event itself.
1633 Broadway, 16th Floor
New York, NY 10019
(212) 708-1600
www.sundancechannel.com

TBS
Offering movies, comedy, and sports programming.
1050 Techwood Dr.
Atlanta, GA 30318
(404) 885-5535
www.tbs.com

TCM
Turner Classic Movies.
1050 Techwood Dr.
Atlanta, GA 30318
(404) 885-5535
www.turnerclassicmovies.com

Telemundo
Spanish language programming.
2470 West 8th Avenue
Hialeah, FL 33010
(305) 884-8200
www.telemundo.com

The Tennis Channel
Programming based on the sport of tennis.
2850 Ocean Park Blvd.
Santa Monica, CA 90405
(310) 314-9400
www.thetennischannel.com

TMC
The Movie Channel.
1633 Broadway
New York, NY 10019
(212) 708-1600
www.showtimeonline.com

TNT
Turner Network Television.
1010 Techwood Dr.
Atlanta, GA 30318
(404) 885-4538
www.tnt.tv

Travel Channel
Network devoted to showing travel destinations all over the world.
7700 Wisconsin Avenue
Bethesda, MD 20814
(301) 986-1999
www.travel.discovery.com

Trinity Broadcast Network (TBN)
Christian network.
2442 Michelle
Tustin, CA 92780
(714) 832-2950
www.tbn.org

Turner South
Television about the southern United States.
1050 Techwood Dr.
Atlanta, GA 30318
(404) 885-2290
www.turnersouth.com

TV Guide Channel
The fastest-growing network of 2004, this channel is the premiere television entertainment network for viewers seeking the latest information on the best programs, hottest stars, and latest trends on TV.
6922 Hollywood Blvd.
Los Angeles, CA 90028
(323) 817-4899

TV Land
1515 Broadway
New York, NY 10036
(212) 258-7500
www.nickatnite.com

TVG (The Interactive Horseracing Network)
Broadcasting live horse races from around the country.
19545 N.W. Von Neumann Drive, Suite 210
Beaverton, OR 97006
1-888-PLAY-TVG
www.tvg.com

Univision
Spanish language programming.
9405 NW 41st
Miami, FL 33178
(305) 471-3900
www.univision.com

UPN
11800 Wilshire Blvd.
Los Angeles, CA 90025
(310) 575-7000
www.upn.com

USA
Entertainment network featuring TV series, movies, sports, and original programming.
1230 Avenue of the Americas
3rd Floor
New York, NY 10020
www.usanetwork.com

VH1
Music videos and original programming. MTV's "older sibling."
1515 Broadway
New York, NY 10036
(212) 258-7500
www.vh1.com

WB
One of the major national networks.
4000 Warner Blvd.
Bldg. 34R
Burbank, CA 91522
www.thewb.com

WE: Women's Entertainment
Cable network showcasing original series, specials, and movies for women.
150 Crossways Park West
Woodbury, NY 11797
(516) 396-3000
www.we-womensentertainment.com

The Weather Channel
Provides weather information for locations worldwide.
300 Interstate North Parkway
Atlanta, GA 30339
(770) 226-0000
www.weather.com

WGN

Chicago-based station that is broadcast nationally.
2501 W. Bradley Place
Chicago, IL 60618
(773) 528-2311
www.wgncable.com

Wisdom Channel

P.O. Box 1546
Bluefield, WV 24701
(304) 323-8000
www.wisdommedia.com

The Word Network

Multi-denominational urban religious programming with both spiritual and educational content.
20733 W. Ten Mile
Southfield, MI 48075
(248) 357-4566
www.thewordnetwork.com

WorldNet TV

Public affairs, information, and cultural television network of the U.S. Department of State, International Broadcasting Bureau.
US Information Agency
330 Independence Ave
Washington, DC 20237
(202) 260-2596
www.ibb.gov/worldnet

YES Network

Yankees games, with pre- and post-game coverage by sportscaster superstars. Talk, magazine, documentary, and live event formats.
The Chrysler Building
405 Lexington Avenue, 36th Floor
New York, NY 10174-3699
(646) 487-3600
www.yesnetwork.com

Consent and Release Form

The purpose of this CONSENT AND RELEASE is to define and govern the relationship between the undersigned guest and XXXXXX (the "Program") and XXXXXX ("the Company"), including all persons and entities acting on behalf of the Program and/or Company.

1. *Definitions.* The following terms shall have the following meanings in this document and all supplemental documents hereto:

"Company" shall include XXXXX Productions (XYZ), XXXXXXX (XYZ).

"Material" means my name, voice, photograph, actions and likeness, and facts about me *and* on *behalf of the estate of any deceased family member for whom I have the authority to act),* including, without limitation, recordings or reproductions of all or portions of, or relating to, my proposed appearance or actual appearance on the Program, whether or not actually used in the Program, and whether or not taped, filmed or photographed on the premises of the Program or anywhere else before or after this form is signed, and specifically including hidden microphone audio and hidden camera video footage.

"Media" means all media now known or hereafter invented, including, without limitation, Interactive Media including CD-ROM and Internet, all forms of television, home video or other display, whether employing digital, analog or light-based transmission or delivery, electronic storage and retrieval, and merchandising (for example, coffee mugs, T-shirts, books, etc.).

"Use" means recording or using for any purpose (including, without limitation, editorial, entertainment, advertising, exhibition, promotion, cross-promotion, merchandising and trade purposes or as part of the Program).

2. *Grant.*

In return for Company's considering, and possibly selecting, me to appear on the Program, I (*on behalf of myself and of the estate of any deceased family member for whom I have the authority* to act hereby grant to the Associated Parties) grant the right to Use in perpetuity throughout the universe the Material in all Media. I understand that Company is not obligated to include me in any program or to telecast any program in which I appear or to engage in any other Uses of the Material. I waive any rights I might have to review, inspect or approve any Use of the Material, or the subject matter(s) raised in any program that may make Use of the Material or the nature or content of any Use of the Material. I hereby acknowledge and fully understand that the grant of rights extended by me to the Associated Parties includes the right to Use and to re-Use the Material, and to authorize others to Use and to re-Use the Material, an unlimited number of times.

3. *False Statements: Program Content.*

I waive any rights I might have to review, inspect, edit, modify or approve (or to request the same from the Associated Parties) the subject matter(s) raised in any program, any use of any Material or the nature or content of any Uses or Media. I recognize that the Program is intended as Internet entertainment, and my participation in the Program is undertaken at my own risk. I have considered the various risks, I expressly waive my rights of privacy as to the matters discussed on the Program, and I acknowledge that I will make no claim of any kind as to or in connection with any emotional or physical distress, difficulty, other adverse reaction or harm arising out of or relating to the Program, or any Revelation or other information, consequence, or effect in connection therewith.

4. *Payment.*

I have not accepted or agreed to accept, and will not accept or agree to accept, directly or indirectly, any money, service or other valuable consideration for my appearance on, or for the inclusion of any matter as part of, the Program from any person, firm or corporation other than Company. Further, I shall not utilize my appearance on the Program as an endorsement, express or implied, for any goods, services or entity.

5. *Release of My Claims and Hold Harmless by Me.*

I RELEASE AND AGREE TO HOLD HARMLESS the Associated Parties from and against any and all claims and/or causes of action which I may have now, or which I may have at any time in the future, including, without limitation, claims and/or causes of action/litigation (I) that arise from my comments, views or opinions expressed on the Program, and/or (ii) for invasion of privacy, defamation, personal injury (including emotional distress), or death, property damage or destruction, or any other claim or cause of action arising out of the production, distribution, telecast, exhibition or promotion of, or my participation or appearance on the Program (specifically including, but not by way of limitation, any advice or treatment offered in connection therewith), or any other Use of any Material in any Media, including (but not limited to) any such claims and/or causes of action resulting from or arising out of the negligence of any of the Associated Parties.

6. *Indemnities and Defense.*

I AGREE TO INDEMNIFY AND DEFEND all Associated Parties against any and all claims and causes of action (including payment of reasonable attorneys' fees and costs incurred whether or not litigation has begun) asserted by any third party, arising out of or related in any way to my appearance on the Program, any Material, or to my breach of this agreement, if such claim or cause of action either is based upon allegations that I acted negligently, intentionally or willfully causing injury to any person, or the property, reputation, or privacy rights of any third party or with reckless disregard for the rights or safety of others, or their property, or involves allegations of violent acts or statements on my part that injured any third party, including another's property, reputation or rights of privacy. I understand and agree that included Company and the Associated Parties shall be entitled to recoup any and all costs incurred by them as a result of any claim or cause of action provided herein.

Agreed and Accepted:
By: _____   _____   _____
                                    Guest Signature   Date

Agreed and Accepted:

_____   _____

Signature   Date

_____

Guest Name Printed

_____

Print Name and Title

_____

Address

_____

City, State, Zip Code

_____

Telephone No.

_____

S.S. Number

Index

A

AFTRA, 134

agent, 6, 87, 102, 109, 120, 134, 148

antenna, 99–100

arrival at studio, 180

assembly, 134

associate director (AD), 135

associate producer (AP), 22–23, 26

audition, 135

Avid, 135

B

Baron, Anat, 126

bay, 135

Betacam, 135

bid, 15, 136

bio, 73–79, 136

Bird (satellite), 136

booker, 21, 26

booking, 137, 161–165

boom, 137

booth, 137

Brand You 50, The, 33

breakdown, 137

breaking news, 137

bullpen, 7

bumpers, 137–138

bump-in, 138

bump-out, 138

C

cable, 99

Cadell, Ava, 34

callback, 138

call sheet, 138

call time, 138

cameraman, 138

cancellation, 162, 171–173

casting department, 23

casting director, 138

Catherine Crier Show, 171–172

About the Author

Jacquie Jordan has been involved in booking, supervising, or producing as many as 10,000+ television guests. Her credits include a full season at *Donny & Marie, Maury, Geraldo,* and *The Montel Williams Show.*

Currently, she is the co-executive producer for AMC's new show, *Sunday Morning Shootout.* Jacquie is a successful national seminar leader and trainer. Her innovative and informative seminars to corporations, such as "Getting Your Idea, Product, or Story on TV," have been recognized by the industry.

For more information and contact info, visit www.JacquieJordan.com.